MARCO POLO

MONTENEGRO

HUNGARY

ROMANIA

Zagreb
CROATIA

Belgrade

BOSNIA AND
HERZEGOVINA

SERBIA

Sarajevo

MONTENEGRO
RKS

Podgorica
Adriatic Sea
ALBANIA

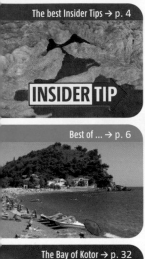

SYMBOLS

INSIDER TIP	Insider Tip
★	Highlight
●●●●	Best of …
☼	Scenic view

**PRICE CATEGORIES
HOTELS**

Expensive	over 70 euros
Moderate	30–70 euros
Budget	under 30 euros

The prices are for two persons in a double room, including breakfast, per night

**PRICE CATEGORIES
RESTAURANTS**

Expensive	over 17 euros
Moderate	12–17 euros
Budget	under 12 euros

The prices are for a meal with a starter, main course, dessert and one beverage

On the cover: Explore the ice-cold Tara by boat p. 83 | The farmers' market in Bar p. 51

CONTENTS

Cetinje, Podgorica ... → p. 64

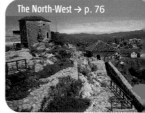
The North-West → p. 76

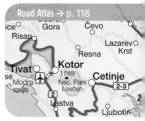
The North-East → p. 84

Road Atlas → p. 118

DID YOU KNOW?

Timeline → p. 12
Local specialities → p. 26
Olives → S. 57
Against the current → p. 62
World-class art in Cetinje → p. 68
Church controversy → p. 83
Budgeting → p. 107
Currency converter → p. 108
Books & Films → p. 109
Weather in Budva → p. 111

MAPS IN THE GUIDEBOOK

(120 A1) Page numbers and coordinates refer to the road atlas
(0) Site/address located off the map. Coordinates are also given for places that are not marked on the road atlas
A street map of Kotor can be found on p. 123, maps of Budva, Cetinje, Herceg Novi and Podgorica can be found inside the back cover

INSIDE BACK COVER:
PULL-OUT MAP →

PULL-OUT MAP 𝄃

(𝄃 A−B 2−3) Refers to the removable pull-out map

The best
MARCO POLO
Insider Tips

Our top 15 Insider Tips

INSIDER TIP **Nudism in the Bojana Delta**
The country's longest nudist beach is located on a beautiful river island → **p. 63**

INSIDER TIP **Feel at home**
Branka and Dragan Vuksanović lived abroad for many years and now welcome guests from around the world with typical Montenegrin hospitality to their lovely holiday apartments → **p. 59**

INSIDER TIP **Angelic voices in the fjord**
Klape are male a capella choirs that sing slow ballads. The best of them perform at a festival held in Perast in August → **p. 103**

INSIDER TIP **A dream in white**
The Rivijera, one of the most beautiful hotels in Montenegro, is located on the picturesque Bay of Petrovac → **p. 59**

INSIDER TIP **Hands-on geography**
The relief map in Cetinje gives a bird's-eye view of Montenegro's mountains (photo above) → **p. 101**

INSIDER TIP **Relaxed wine tasting**
You can taste top quality wines at the Sjekloća Vino estate at your leisure → **p. 74**

INSIDER TIP **Ruins with a view**
Montenegro's rulers once resided in Žabljak on Lake Skadar. Today, there is a splendid view far across the landscape from the ruins of the castle → **p. 75**

INSIDER TIP **Window on nature**
See the great diversity of the highland flora in the botanical gardens in Kolašin→ **p. 101**

INSIDER TIP **Carnival in Kotor**
Young and old jesters take over the city twice a year – in February and in August (photo right) → **pp. 102, 103**

BEST OF ...

FOR FREE

● *Window shopping with the rich and beautiful*
Partiti oči (to get teary eyes) is how the Montenegrins describe window shopping. The loveliest place for this is in *Porto Montenegro* where the best – and most expensive – boutiques offer an insight into the world of the rich and beautiful. It costs nothing to look ... → p. 45

● *A clan in the museum*
The poet Marko Miljanov immortalised the militant Kuči clan in his historical work. You will be able to immerse yourself in the life of the writer and the history of the clan in the *Miljanov Museum* in Medunda. Entrance is free → p. 75

● *Scenic road instead of a tunnel*
You will save yourself some distance but will have to pay 2.50 euros if you drive through the Sozina Tunnel from Lake Skadar to the Montenegrin coast. The alternative route is via the winding *road from Virpazar on the Adriatic near Petrovac*; it is free and offers panoramic vistas → p. 50

● *Montenegro's up-and-coming artists*
This is the place to discover new talent! The *Gallery in Herceg Novi*, one of the oldest in the country, exhibits work by young Montenegrin artists. You don't have to pay to have a look at them → p. 35

● *A free bench at the beach*
A sun lounger on the beach in *Petrovac* costs 10 euros; a place on one of the lovely old benches on the promenade is gratis. You will still have the sand and sea right in front of you and trees to provide shade (photo) → p. 58

● *Collect herbs*
Mint, thyme, rocket and nettles – all of the fragrant herbs of Montenegro are on sale at the country's markets. But it is much more fun to pick them yourself! So head off to the hinterland of Lake Skadar and get away from the main roads! The herbs grow wild near *Donji Brčeli* and *Gornji Ceklin* and many other places → p. 95

●●●● Dots in guidebook refer to 'Best of ...' tips

ONLY IN MONTENEGRO
Unique experiences

● *Christmas Eve in January*

According to the Julian calendar, *Christmas Eve* falls on 24 December, but the Gregorian calendar has it on 6 January. The churches are packed on that day and the old rites are celebrated in clouds of incense. The *badnjak*, an oak branch that is supposed to bring luck and happiness, takes the place of a Christmas tree (photo) → **p. 102**

● *Monument on the summit*

The Montenegrins revere their national heroes with great fervour and they have placed a colossal monument to the greatest on one of the highest mountains in the country. The poet Prince Njegoš has found his final resting place in the *mausoleum,* with spectacular views, on the Jezerski vrh summit on Mount Lovćen → **p. 92**

● *Trees full of obituary notices*

Obituaries are pinned to trees in Montenegro. The white sheets of paper in their blue frames transform death into a surreal work of art. They can be found wherever people congregate such as on the *Trg Bećir Bega Osmanagića* square in the Stara Varoš district in Podgorica → **p. 71**

● *Our daily bread*

No meal is complete without it: white bread is the staple food of the Montenegrins. The loaves that are subsidised by the state are known as *narodni hleb* (people's bread) and are rather bland. However, the bread the famers' wives in the north bake is pure bliss! Enjoy it yourself at the *Razvršje Camping Site* where the owner's mother bakes her own → **p. 81**

● *Chequered history and testimonies in stone*

The fate of the small country has repeatedly been determined by European powers. These cultural influences are immediately apparent in the impressive architecture of *Kotor's old town* → **p. 41**

● *Try your luck?*

Casinos are a special branch of tourism in Montenegro. All self respecting hotels have one and the best guests are the Italians who jet across the Adriatic at the weekend and leave their money in the country – much to the delight of the locals. Would you like to do what they do and see if you are any better? One place where you can try your luck is in the hotel *Maestral in Pržno* → **p. 56**

ONLY IN

BEST OF ...

● *In an Orthodox monastery*

The Metropolitan Bishop of Herzegovina had the *Ostrog Monastery* built into the cliff as a place of refuge from the Turks. If you seek shelter from the rain here, you will find peace in the tranquil rooms and fascinating frescoes on stone (photo) → **p. 79**

● *Brave raindrops on the sand*

Walking barefoot along the beach and having your feet massaged by the wet sand – the mild climate of the Adriatic makes it possible for you to do this with or without an umbrella; try it on the *Grand Beach* in Ulcinj → **p. 62**

● *Centre of modern art*

Most Montenegrin artists' have a style that is in character with their country: full of power, energy and colour. That makes it impossible to think of the rain outside! The *Centar savremene umjetnosti Crne Gore* in Podgorica displays contemporary art → **p. 70**

● *Silver screen dreams*

Enjoy Montenegro's lively cinematic landscape on a rainy evening. The *Kino Kultura* in Podgorica shows foreign films in their original language. The film director Emir Kusturica is the owner of the venerable *Hotel Aurora* in Herceg Novi. Watching one the classics in the hotel's beautiful cinema is a special treat → **pp. 72, 38**

● *Cheese instead of rain*

Hop into your car and set off on a culinary journey. Take the *cheese tour* and savour all of the country's specialities. That should take care of more than one rainy day → **p. 87**

● *Museum to seafarers*

The area around the Bay of Kotor is the birthplace of many famous captains who braved the wind and weather on the high seas. You can be inspired by their feats in the *Maritime Museum* in Kotor → **p. 41**

RAIN

RELAX AND CHILL OUT
Take it easy and spoil yourself

● *Tranquil cloister at the end of the world*
A day on God's soil: take a boat ride to *Beška Island* where a handful of nuns lead a life of seclusion. You will be able to find peace of mind and think over all you have experienced on your trip in the small church or by just looking at the wild pomegranates (photo) → **p. 73**

● *Luxurious oasis of relaxation*
Take in the view of the mountains around the Bay of Kotor from the swimming pool, enjoy a massage or just relax while the waves lap against the yachts in the sea only a few metres away – the *Purobeach* in Tivat offers luxury relaxation → **p. 46**

● *Broom in bloom on the coast*
When the broom is in bloom at the end of May, the coast road meaders through a sea of yellow. Find a pleasant spot on the peaceful bay of *Dobra Voda*, lay down on your picnic blanket and enjoy the enchanting sight → **p. 52**

● *Sea breeze and massage*
The changing winds and the long, pristine bay in Buljarica are a tonic for the lungs and the owner of the small *Savojo Hotel* will take care of any back pains with a massage on the beach → **p. 60**

● *The place for a browse*
Trg Nikole Đurkovića in Herceg Novi, which was once known as Salt Square, is the perfect place for relaxed holiday reading: the tiny *So* bookshop also has a large selection of foreign titles. After you have finished browsing, you can go to one of the many bars around the square, sip a cup of coffee under a sunshade and immerse yourself in your new purchase → **p. 37**

● *Wellness with tradition*
The team of doctors and physiotherapists in the *Institut Igalo* have been taking care of their guests for more than six decades. Mud packs and aromatherapy are just two of the items on offer → **p. 39**

INTRODUCTION

DISCOVER MONTENEGRO!

So close and yet so far: the state of Montenegro is only a few hours flying time from London, Edinburgh or Dublin. The land of the Black Mountain (Monte Negro), the land of heroes and pirates that drove the Turks out of the mountains and raided Venetian ships in the Middle Ages, is still relatively unknown. Montenegro's coastal strip is not even 300km/186mi long and swimmers have only 70km/43mi of beach available for their pleasure; the other half of the country is dominated by the mountains at an altitude of over 1000m/3281ft above sea level. Raging rivers wind their way through the deep canyons of the Durmitor and Bjelasica mountain ranges. Snow-covered peaks are reflected in tiny alpine lakes. The Montenegrins have buried their most famous poet Petar II Petrović Njegoš on one of the countless mountain ranges, the Lovćen, and from his burial site there are panoramic views all the way to Bosnia, Croatia, Albania and – on a clear day – across the Adriatic to Italy.

The distance between the most westerly and easterly points in Montenegro is a mere 176km/109mi and the country measures only 200km/124mi from north to south.

Photo: Budva

The railway line between Belgrade and Bar is one of the most spectacular in the Balkans

However, it is rare to have so much to see and experience in such a small area. After the Grand Canyon, the Tara River Canyon in the north-west of the country is the deepest in the world and one of the last primeval forests in Europe lies hidden in the highlands in the Biogradska gora National Park. More birds nest on Lake Skadar than on any other in Europe and the only fjord in the Mediterranean lies beneath almost perpendicular rock faces between the towns of Herceg Novi and Kotor. And, nowhere else on the eastern Adriatic are there more beautiful sandy beaches than between Bar and Ulcinj.

> **Rarely can one experience so much in such a small area**

The idyllic bays hidden behind rocks and lined with pines, cypresses and olive trees are typical of Montenegro's coastline. A stroll through the flower town of Herceg Novi,

the seafaring hamlet of Perast or across the picturesque hotel island of Sveti Stefan will take you back to the heyday of European architecture. The pedestrian area of the old town of Kotor reveals an architectural melange of Venetian Baroque buildings and Austro-Hungarian town houses. Centuries-old Orthodox monasteries are tucked away further inland.

The Montenegrins defend the country's multicultural spirit, which continued to flourish here after the collapse of Josip Broz Tito's Socialist Yugoslavia, with great fervour. Croats, Serbs, Albanians, Roma and Muslims have lived alongside each other for centuries – and both the government and opposition of the small republic stress the virtue of this tolerance in their efforts to accede to the European Union. The Montenegrins have no doubt that their country's roots can be found deep in Europe: you will discover traces of the rich history of this small country wherever you go. In Cetinje, the old embassy buildings recall the time when the daughters of Tsar Nicholas I married into the major courts of Europe and the wily diplomat was known as the 'father-in-law of Europe' – an appropriate title for a man with nine daughters!

> **The Montenegrins defend their multicultural spirit with great élan**

Well before that, noble families from Venice to Petersburg had invited Montenegrin artists and captains into their employ. And, the European roots sink even deeper: Greeks, Illyrians and Romans settled in the area south of Dubrovnik before the Roman Empire divided its territory at the end of the 4th century. After that, the border between East and West Rome ran directly below the Bay of Kotor. Today, most of the Catholics

1878
The Congress of Berlin recognises Montenegro as a sovereign, independent state

1918
Independence ends with defeat in the First World War. Montenegro becomes part of the new Kingdom of Serbs, Croats and Slovenes

Second World War
Italian troops occupy Montenegro in 1941. Under the leadership of Milovan Đilas, Montenegrin partisans join Tito's revolt against the occupying forces. Montenegro is liberated in 1944

of Croatian nationality live in this area – as well as near the border with Croatia and Bosnia. A total of around 3.5 per cent of Montenegro's population are Catholic, 16 per cent Muslim and the majority – almost 73 per cent – are members of the Eastern Orthodox Church. The first Jewish community in Montenegro was established in the year 2011: it has exactly 100 members.

The country had a long wait before once again regaining its independence. In 1878, the Congress of Berlin recognised the Kingdom of Montenegro as a sovereign state. Crna Gora remained independent until 1918 but pro-Serbian forces prevailed when the first Kingdom of Serbs, Croats and Slovenes was proclaimed. Montenegro was also included when Tito established the Socialist Federal Republic of Yugoslavia in 1945. Among the six Yugoslav constituent states, Montenegro always brought up the rear in economic terms. Many people emigrated to Western Europe or the United States in search of work and it was not until the 1960s that Montenegro's potential as a holiday destination was discovered. And then things really took off. Anybody who had a spare bed rented it to a tourist.

> **The country had a long wait before becoming independent again**

Hotels with 'beguiling socialist charm' sprang up everywhere. Sveti Stefan, the fishing island carved out of stone, became an exclusive holiday location for celebrities such as Sophia Loren and Michael Douglas.

However, the boom did not last long. The Yugoslavian war in the 1990s crippled the entire economy. Although there was no action in the country itself, Montenegro suffered from the uncertain political situation in the Balkans: the once popular holiday destination for Europeans fell out of favour. Hotels and guesthouses went fell into disrepair and poverty once again hit the country that had relied so much on tourism and many young university graduates went abroad to find work.

Many politicians felt that the confederation with Serbia was an obstacle on Montenegro's path into the European Union. Milo Đukanović, who was president from 1998 to 2002 and Prime Minister several times after that, did everything he could to promote secession. He introduced the euro as the country's currency in 2002

1992
Proclamation of the Federal Republic of Yugoslavia, consisting of Serbia and Montenegro

2006
Montenegro withdraws from the Serbia-Montenegro confederation

2009
The country applies for NATO membership

2010
Montenegro becomes a candidate for European Union accession

2012
The European Union decides to start accession negotiations with Montenegro

Hot spot for well-heeled visitors to the Adriatic: the luxurious Porto Montenegro Marina in Tivat

and established borders within the state of Serbia-Montenegro. A narrow majority (55 per cent) voted for independence from Serbia in a referendum.

The new state was born on 3 June 2006 but soon developed teething problems: the transition from socialism to capitalism proved a difficult one. The privatisation of state-owned enterprises usually failed and a high unemployment was the result. However, the elite continued to live in a grand style – and they still do. Milo Đukanović's fortune is estimated at several million euros. At the same time, accusations of corruption were raised against the political and economic establishment. Italy carried out investigations against Đukanović; he was said to be directly involved in cigarette smuggling in the 1990s. That seemed to have no harm on his career; his party won the 2012 elections and he became Prime Minister once again. Joining the European Union remains this government's goal. Following the decision to start accession negotiations, this goal appears to be within reach but it is uncertain how long the process will take.

Looking beyond any economic and political difficulties Montenegro is still a wonderful holiday destination for dreamers and adventurers. The country attracts tourist with its 'Wild Beauty' slogan and visitors

> **Montenegro has remained a country for dreamers and adventurers**

can indeed still discover many unsoiled landscapes. And to top it off, the hospitality of the 625,000 Montenegrins is legendary.

WHAT'S HOT

1

Only the sky above us

Open air On the coast you can hear the clinking of glasses – open air bars are a hot trend around Budva. The place to see and be seen is the *Trocadero Red (Mediteranska, www. trocaderoclub.com)*. Although the *Hacienda Bar (Mediteranska, www.haciendabarbudva.com)* is not on the sea but in the old town, the palm trees and straw thatch will make you feel like you are at the beach. There is even more of a summer mood at the annual music festival: *Summer Fest (www. summerfest.me)*.

Art generation

2

Art Montenegro's art scene is enjoying its up-and-coming stars. One of them is Igor Rakcevic *(photo)*, whose works are on display in the *Pizana Gallery (Porto Montenegro, Tivat)*. His works out of everyday objects such as his 'Spinning Bottles' are fascinating. The creations of Ivanka Prelevic and the graduates of the renowned *Faculty of Arts of the Crne Gore (Vojvode Batrića 1, Cetinje, www.ucg.ac.me)* are also worth closer inspection. Another tip is the Spinnaker Gallery in Herceg Novi *(Sveta Bubala 2)*. You can even spend the night there.

Architectural nature

3

Hand in hand with nature There is a great deal of construction taking place in Montenegro – and some innovative projects are also environmentally friendly. The *UN Eco Building (www.un.org.me)* in Podgorica was designed by the architect Daniel Fügenschuh *(www.fuegenschuh.at)* and sets a new benchmark: it is the world's first completely sustainable UN building. The private projects *Seagarden (Kotor, photo)* and *Mimosa (Kumbor)* are also good examples – and show that aesthetics, comfort and environmental protection are not mutually exclusive.

Sweet dreams

Overnight A guest of the queen? That is easily arranged in Montenegro. The *Queen of Montenegro (Narodnog fronta, Bečići, www.queenofmontenegro.com, photo)* is a spacious and stylish hotel with a swimming pool with a sea view. The *Astoria (Njegoševa 4, www. budva.astoriamontenegro.com)*, with its six rooms and six suites, is located in the old town of Budva. The terrace overlooking the Adriatic is especially charming while in Kolašin there is the *Hotel Lipka (Mojkovačka 20, www.adriastar-hotels. com)*, a contemporary design of stone, glass and wood. After a day skiing or hiking guests can relax here in the Turkish bath or have a massage with essential oils.

Staying power

Extreme Montenegro is an ideal country for endurance sports enthusiasts. Long-distance hiking trails, extreme cycle and swimming trips are the latest trends. The latter is offered by the British tour operator *Swimtrek (www.swimtrek.com)*. The guided tour makes its way through the Bay of Kotor past the islands around Perast, through lakes such as Lake Skadar and – naturally – into the famous Blue Grotto. Those who prefer a bicycle saddle should get in touch with *Hooked on Cycling (www.hookedoncycling. co.uk)*. The team travels along Montenegro's coast on bicycles and by sailing ship. Hikers can explore the *Transversal Route* in the coastal mountains on their own. The 182km/113mi long-distance award winning trail is still an insiders' tip.

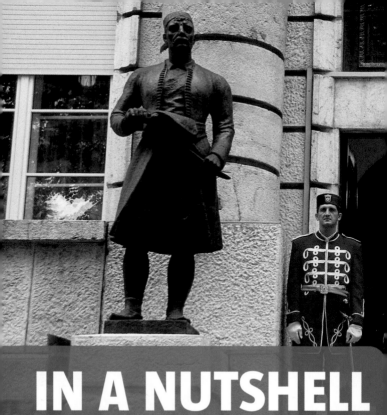

IN A NUTSHELL

CRNA GORA

Hardly anybody outside of the country knows the country's real name: Crna Gora (Black Mountain). Although that is the exact translation of Montenegro, discussions still take place in the country over what is more important: a name that has existed for more than 500 years that almost no foreigner can pronounce or one known worldwide. At least the official tourism organisation has settled on Montenegro as more effective in international advertising.

ECO STATE

In 1991 Montenegro's parliament proclaimed the country as an Ecological State but in reality it only exists on paper. This is the verdict of the NGO Green Home *(www. greenhome.co.me)* that investigates environmental issues. The lack of interest shown by the government institutions responsible for environmental protection is the greatest problem. Natural resources are being ruthlessly destroyed and fertile land turned into building sites. The construction of waterworks on the Tara could only be prevented by a human chain that picketed for many days.

The government's indifference is particularly apparent along the coast: the enormous water consumption by the large

Photo: The Presidential Palace in Cetinje

National heroes, the Habsburg rule and 'Mother Russia': Montenegro's past is reflected in its present

hotels leads to shortages every summer; the daily traffic jam on the coast roads is often several miles long. Many efforts are currently being made to try to solve these problems. Roads are being built and the water supply improved. But, even so environmental protection often falls by the wayside. Development of the Luštica Peninsula is planned and there are even schemes to 'open up' the majestic Durmitor and Bjelasica mountain ranges. Montenegro's nature conservation organisations are fighting these projects but the final outcome remains uncertain.

A measure which the government stated was aimed at supporting environmental protection projects was withdrawn in the spring of 2012 and the eco tax on all cars entering the country is no longer being levied.

HABSBURGS

The old Austro-Hungarian embassy in Cetinje is probably the most obvious expression of the more than 100 years of splendid rule by the dual monarchy in Montenegro. Or, to be more precise, in parts of Montenegro. In 1815, the Congress of Vienna only granted the Habsburg Empire the area around the Bay of Kotor to the south of Budva. The Austro-Hungarian region reached as far as Cetinje for a short time at the beginning of the 19th century before the Russians and then the French sent in their troops. After the defeat of Napoleon, Habsburg rule lasted into the First World War because the 1878 Congress of Berlin had placed the coastline under Austrian command. The Habsburgs left not only architectural traces: many words – such as *palačinka* (pancakes), *escajg* (cutlery) and *paradajz* (tomato) – have found their way into everyday vocabulary.

HEROISM AND HONOUR

Čojstvo i junaštvo – honour and heroism have always been at the top of the list of virtues in the patriarchal society of Montenegro. There are monuments celebrating heroic deeds on every corner. When the Turks controlled the Balkans, they were unable to subject the people living in the mountainous north – and so the legend of the untamed mountain princes was born. Even today, each Montenegrin man knows which clan *(pleme)* and which brotherhood *(bratsvo)* he belongs to. One of the largest clans, the Kuči, lives in Medun near Podgorica and it even has a museum devoted to it. The day of the family's patron saint is the most important feast day for any Orthodox Montenegrin. Once a year, a lavish celebration is held with friends and the family after the priest has blessed the house and property. This goes hand in hand with monotone heroic songs accompanied the sound of the folk instrument, the *gusle*. The *gusle* player, the *guslar*, not only plays old pieces of music but also writes new numbers celebrating courageous deeds. This music is particularly popular in the north of the country but tourists might find it a bit difficult to get used to.

JEWISH COMMUNITY

Montenegro's first Jewish community was founded in autumn 2011; its 100 members making it the smallest in the world at the time. In the spring of 2012, Judaism was officially recognised as the state's fourth religion. About 200 Jews live in Montenegro, most of them are from inter-faith families in which only the mother was Jewish.

The mediaeval Jewish cemetery in the Bay of Kotor is one of the few testimonies to centuries of secular Jewish life in the country. It was in a miserable state until 2005 when its restoration was undertaken with the support of the Kotor town authorities. The history of Montenegrin Jews began at the time of the Inquisition in the 15th century when Sephardic Jews were forced to leave Spain and Portugal and settled in the Balkans. 62,000 of the 80,000 Jews living in the former Kingdom of Yugoslavia lost their lives during the Holocaust. The few Montenegrin Jews fled to Albania where the majority managed to survive. There is currently no synagogue in Montenegro; there is no money and it is unsure when it will be possible to build a house of worship. In any case, there are not enough men to celebrate a service in the synagogue. There are only seven male Jews with Jewish mothers and the required number is nine.

LANGUAGE

A constitutional decree introduced Montenegrin as the national language after the foundation of the new state; until then Serbian was the official language. There are actually only minimal differences between the grammar and vocabulary of the two languages. The Montenegrin word for river is *rijeka* and the Serbian equivalent *rejka*; world is *svijet* instead of *svet* and morning *sjutra* in place of *sutra*. The expressions *dobar dan* (good day) and *hvala* (thank you) are the same in both languages.

The question of who speaks which language divides the country and has become a political issue. According to the 2011 census, 36 per cent of the population communicate in Montenegrin and 42 per cent Serbian. That is why the latter demands more rights for their language such as school lessons in Serbian in areas where the majority of the pupils speak that language. This is the case in the north of the country. But, it is not only a matter of the language. Many Montenegrins call themselves Serbs and feel that they belong to that nation. Today, around 100,000 Montenegrins still live in the Serbian capital Belgrade which is the unofficial second largest Montenegrin city. However, the newly-founded Montenegrin state has the aim of stressing and boosting everything 'Montenegrin' – including the language as part of the national identity. This dispute has been continuing for years and has still not been settled. The 5 per cent Albanians in the country have it easier: bilingualism is prescribed by law in the south and north-east of the country where Albanian is also spoken. This can be seen on the road signs: for example, the city Ulcinj is also shown as Ulqin.

NJEGOŠ, THE POET PRINCE

Prince Bishop Petar II Petrović Njegoš (1813–51) is possibly the most multitalented personality in Montenegrin history.

He died of tuberculosis at an early age but managed to not only reform the tiny state's outdated political system with its antiquated clan structures (and by doing so brought the country closer to Europe), but also to write the most significant work in Southern Slavic literature 'The Mountain Wreath' *(Gorski Vjenac)*. A work remained

In the mausoleum on Mount Lovćen

required reading throughout the former Yugoslavia until the start of the Balkan wars. The subject is the heroic struggle of his predecessor Danilo I to liberate the country from the Turks and – the other side of the coin – the murder of thousands of Islam converts. Njegoš wrote down many of the verses, which have their roots in popular poetry, for the first time in the 'The Mountain Wreath' and in so doing significantly brought forward the standardization of the written language. One line of his work is as follows: 'When things go well 'tis easy to be good/in suffering one learns who the real hero is'. Njegoš'

The unspoiled wilderness of the Durmitor Mountains

final resting place is in a large mausoleum on Mount Lovćen, Montenegro's 'Olympus' that is easily visible from the coast as well as the highlands.

RAIN

Tourists are hardly give the rain a thought when they bathe in dazzling sunshine on the coast from March to October. But, in spring and late autumn a few wet days sneak in and revive the withered plants. However, Montenegrin rain is rather special: it does not last long but makes up for that by being all the heavier. As soon as it starts, the mountain streams gush directly into the sea, it becomes dark, the white-crested waves smash against the shore, there is thunder and lightning and heavy raindrops beat down on the earth – and five minutes later, it's all over. The fragrance of plants and flowers lingers, the air is sharp and clear, the sun shines again – but only for five minutes and then the spectacle begins once more. This is particularly violent in the mountainous north of the country with its thunder and lightning storms and masses of water pouring down from the heavens. Anybody who experiences such a day of rain will never forget the force of the elements and the smells and colours of nature.

REAL ESTATE

The sale of land on Montenegro's coast seems to be over: any locals who owned property near the Adriatic sold it to make money. The prices exploded in 2008 after a law was passed that made it possible for foreign land owners to register their property under their own name. A square metre of living space in the best locations cost as much as 3000 euros. It is estimated that 3700 acres now belong to foreigners. Serbs are traditionally at the top of the list, followed closely by the Russians who have their *dachas* in Montenegro. In the mean time, prices have fallen but construction is still taking place. Lavish villas and luxury hotels have been built on the beaches and block access to the coast. The construction boom between Budva and Sveti Stefan has transformed the most beautiful beaches in Montenegro into rows of nondescript hotels. However, not all building work has been completed and a huge residential complex on the Bay of Zavalais the largest

abandoned building ruin in the region. In 2012, high-level politicians from Budva were sentenced for illegal wheeling and dealing in Zavala and received prison sentences.

RUSSIANS

The Montenegrins have always loved *Majka Rusija,* (Mother Russia) and there are historical reasons for their enthusiasm. The Tsar's soldiers fought side by side with the locals during the wars against the Turks in the 19th century and Stalin was admired by the Montenegrin Communists even after Tito had broke with the Soviet Union. Today this loyalty has been reciprocated by the Russians who have declared Montenegro to be their second homeland. There are Russian real estate agents everywhere in the country selling housing estates to their countrymen. There are 10,000 Russians living in Budva alone. They listen to local Russian radio stations, their grandchildren attend Russian schools. Russian investors have put their money – more or less successfully – into the Montenegrin economy and around 300,000 Russian tourists visited Montenegro in 2012; that

is an impressive number in a country that only has a population of 625,000.

WOMEN

The image of the beautiful, intelligent Montenegrin woman was established a good 100 years ago by the four daughters of the last King of Montenegro Nikola. Elena and Zorka became queens of Italy and Yugoslavia and Anastazia and Milica lived at the Russian court. However, most other Montenegrins did not enjoy such a comfortable existence. Life was no bed of roses in their archaic male dominated society. In the 1960s, women were still expected to walk a few steps behind their husbands as a sign of respect. Their role in everyday life was limited to taking care of the children and working in the kitchen. Things have finally changed in the 21st century. Young, well-educated, self-confident Montenegrin women in particular are slowly making changes to the man's world. In addition, it is becoming increasingly common to find successful women in politics and business. One such example is the 53-year-old Milica Pejanovic-Đurišič who was named Minister of Defence in 2012 after a long career in politics.

Ljiljana Raičević founded the women's refuge *(Sigurna ženska kuća)* in the capital city Podgorica in 1999 and helped countless women who had escaped from their violent husbands. The 65-year-old takes every opportunity she has to denounce the inflexible structures of everyday life. In 2006, Amnesty International awarded her a prize for her efforts. In remote villages in the mountainous regions such as Tušine near Šavnik one still finds relics from the days when men were supposedly worth more than women: *virganas* the so-called 'the third sex'. Women who have to live as men if the family does not have a son and heir. They do not marry, take care of the house and farm and dress like men.

FOOD & DRINK

The country might be small but the variety of culinary delights is enormous! And most of it comes from the Montenegro's abundant natural resources. Contented cows graze on the mountain slopes and in the valleys. Mushrooms and wild herbs, such as mint and thyme, grow off the main highways. There are olive groves and avenues of fig trees, and vegetables out of the garden in summer. And, you simply have to try the fresh fish *(riba)* caught in Lake Skadar and the waters of the Adriatic.

You can savour it grilled *(na žaru)*, boiled *(lešo)* or as a stew *(brodeto)* in many restaurants and pubs. But even the fresh salad seafood *(riblja salata)*, stuffed squid from the grill *(punjeni lignji na žaru)* or mussels in white wine, parsley and olive oil *(mušule buzara)* are all comparable to the dishes prepared by the Italian chefs on the other side of the Adriatic. Almost all of the restaurants in Budva, Herceg Novi and Risan also offer risotto *(rižot)* – served with squid, seafood or shrimp. But you will not only find traces of Italian cuisine in the harbour cities: pasta and pizza in all variants can be found in the Durmitor Mountains in the far north of the country.

Montenegro's second major culinary district is located between the coast and the

Photo: *Njeguški pršut* (air dried ham) and smoked sausages

Culinary specialities ranging from fish to game: light Mediterranean fare on the coast and hearty farm dishes in the mountains

mountains and characterised by the wealth of fish in Lake Skadar. This is where you will find eel, carp and bleak on your plate – grilled, dried, boiled, smoked or pan-fried. You can also enjoy many of these fish specialities in the restaurants in the capital city, Podgorica.

With the possible exception of trout (*pastrmka*) and carp, the realm of fish in the frying pan or pot ends in Podgorica.

Meat takes over – and the cooking in the higher regions around Kolašin, Žanljak and Nikšić is correspondingly hearty. Everything the pastures and farms produces finds its way to the plate – high-quality natural ingredients that will not only appeal to fans of organic food. You should try lamb that is baked under a *sač*, a large metal or ceramic bell shaped lid covered with ashes and live coals. The

LOCAL SPECIALITIES

BEVERAGES

▶ **Krstač** – full-bodied, dry white wine
▶ **Nikšićko pivo** – *the* Montenegrin beer
▶ **Vranac Pro Corde** – the best red wine; good for the heart

FOOD

▶ **balšića tava** – strips of veal topped with a sauce of eggs, milk and cream
▶ **bokeljski brodet** – fish stew with sprats, anchovies or similar small fish simmered in a broth of onions, white wine, parsley, olive oil and garlic
▶ **crni rižot** – risotto coloured black by squid ink
▶ **imam bajeldi** – baked aubergine with a tomato, garlic and onion mixture
▶ **jagnjetina u mlijeku** – lamb cooked in milk and then browned

▶ **kačamak** – cheesy Montenegrin polenta; made with corn flour like its Italian counterpart
▶ **kajmak** – fresh creamy cheese similar to clotted cream (photo left)
▶ **krap u tavu** – carp cooked in a pan and served with prunes, apples and quince (photo right)
▶ **njeguška šnicla** – breaded pork escalope stuffed with *kajmak*, ham and sheep milk cheese
▶ **paštrovski makaruli** – noodles made with whole wheat flour served with olive oil and cheese preserved in brine
▶ **pastrmka u kiselom mlijeku** – trout in yogurt; eaten cold
▶ **priganice** – fried pastry served with honey, similar to a donut
▶ **riblja juha** – fish soup
▶ **sir u ulju** – sheep milk cheese preserved in olive oil

best place to enjoy this is in a traditional round wooden hut *(savardak)*. The *njeguški pršut* (air dried ham) and *njeguški sir*, which is similar to ricotta, come from the village of the same name, Njeguši, between Cetinje and Kotor. These delicacies are offered in small family-run *konobas* (taverns) by the roadside. They are served with a thick slice of bread that each family bakes in a wood-burning stove following its own recipe and a glass of *medovina* (old Slavic honey drink) and you will be able to relax and enjoy a unique view of the Lovćen Mountains. Another special treat is the fresh goat's cheese *mladi kozji sir*. The best is produced in the Kolašin region in the north-east.

No meal in Montenegro would be complete without bread. The *narodni hleb* is the traditional loaf: all bakeries are required to have a stock of this so-called 'people's bread', which is subsidised by the state and only costs the equivalent of around 0.50 euros. However, the bread is somewhat bland.

This is made up for by the delicious traditional turnovers *(pita)*: sheets of *jufka* pastry filled with cheese *(sirnica)*, spinach *(zeljanica)* or meat *(burek)* and accompanied by a glass of yogurt. Typical types of Balkan fast-food are *ćevapčići*, spicy meat rolls served with chips and raw onions, and *pljeskavica* (hamburger). You can buy them at kiosks wherever you are in the country.

Sometime a salad is all you will need on a hot summer day: the summer vegetables smell and taste heavenly. The *šopska salata* includes tomatoes, cucumber, onions and peppers topped with sheep milk cheese. *Kupus salata* is another delicacy: shredded cabbage with black olives in a light vinaigrette made with olive oil.

Those with a sweet tooth will have a hard time in Montenegro. There are no afternoon tea cakes and none of the classic pastries that are common in Western Europe. One solution can be found on the menu of the better restaurants: the *palačinke* (pancakes) the Austrians brought to Montenegro. The classic pancakes are filled with nuts or jam but there is a modern variety with Nutella, which is known as *eurokrem* here. With some luck, you might also find apple strudel *(štrudla od jabuka)* or plum cake *(pita od šljiva)* on the menu. Although many varieties of fruit grow in Montenegro, fruit salad *(voćna salata)* is rarely offered in restaurants. Ice cream *(sladoled)* is much more common. Tourists who risk the ori-

ental *baklawa* (puff pastry stuffed with nuts and raisins) should not overlook the glass of water served with it: it will help them swallow the sticky pastry. The various jams and marmalades that are sold

Typical Montenegrin delicacies: *prijatno!*

at the markets and in the supermarkets are far too sweet for most tourists' taste. However, fig jam *(marmelada od smokve)* is a really tasty speciality.

If you like hard liquor, you should also try the local spirits. While plum brandy *šljivovica* is the favourite in the north, people on the coast prefer the Montenegrin grappa variety known as *loza* (with an alcoholic content of over 45 per cent). Both are available throughout the country and there are now many small distilleries that produce excellent brandies. *Loza* and *šljivovica* are often taken with a mocha or espresso.

Now you're set: bon appétit *(prijatno)* and cheers *(živeli)*!

SHOPPING

A visit to a market in Montenegro is a very special experience; most are held from the morning to the early afternoon. The farmers' markets in the cities are a real treat: fragrant, colourful local produce lies spread out in all its splendour on wooden tables. The farmers' market in Bar on the Adriatic is especially worth a visit.

In addition, each village has a market where all kinds of other goods are sold. Sometimes a farmers' market is also part of this and it is usually cheerful, loud and – above all – inexpensive. Every visitor to Montenegro should experience the spectacle at least once. One of the most beautiful is the INSIDER TIP *market in Tuzi*, a small village between Podgorica and the Albanian border. A shopping spree here is a must if you are in the area. Inexpensive clothing (but watch out for fake designer brands!), hats made of fabric and leather, brooches with shells and wooden beer mugs are all sold at the market.

One oddity has managed to survive since Montenegro's socialist days: shoe shops, supermarkets, pubs and hotels still have a *knjiga utisaka*, (the book of impressions). Customers are supposed to evaluate their shopping experience in it – positive comments are gladly received!

ARTS AND CRAFTS

The long winter evenings in the mountains in the north are the time for wood carving, knitting and crocheting. In former times, the mountain villages were snowed in from December to March and traditional handicrafts helped people pass the time and provided a lot of useful articles for the whole clan. Today, small families have also become more common in Montenegro but hand-crafted goods are still produced – for the tourists. The small works of art are sold directly in front of the house where large bowls decorated with floral motifs or simple boards and cutlery of all sizes await their purchasers. Wooden articles are offered at the markets and in the souvenir shops. But it is best to ignore those made of teak – they are cheap imports.

The wool pullovers might not be exactly haute couture but they are warm and cosy – and sometimes a bit scratchy. The reason is that the wool is not impregnated with any chemicals. Blouses and dresses em-

Shopping Montenegrin style: the markets offer home-made products, fruit and vegetables grown locally, arts and crafts, and kitsch

broidered by hand and crocheted table cloths are becoming increasingly difficult to find; cheap competition from Asia has reached Montenegro in this area as well.

FASHION

There is a wide choice of fashion shops in Montenegro. There are elegant glass and marble boutiques selling exclusive brands such as Prada and Jil Sander and Italian shoes in chic Porto Montenegro. However, at the markets you can buy breezy cotton summer dresses for a mere 10 euros and local designer clothing is sold in the fashion boutiques in the old towns of Budva, Kotor, Herceg Novi and Podgorica. Long dresses with wide sleeves – many of the pieces have been inspired by traditional costumes and based on old patterns and quite a few are also decorated with ornaments made with silver or gold threads.

ICONS

You will not only be able to purchase pictures of Orthodox saints at the various markets but also in the souvenir shops at the monasteries in the country. They do not cost very much and are colourful and rather beautiful. But, be careful if you are offered 'really old' icons – they will be expensive and almost certainly fake.

SILVER JEWELLERY

Tourists who are interested in the filigree works of the local silversmiths will find any number of inexpensive silver necklaces, rings and bracelets in Ulcinj on the Albanian border. Many of the shops are located on *Ulca zlatara*; the name is somewhat confusing as it means 'street of the goldsmiths'.

THE PERFECT ROUTE

ALONG THE ADRIATIC COAST

The tour begins with a stroll through ① *Herceg Novi* → p. 34, the town of mimosa blossoms and promenades. The route from here runs along the coast through small villages until you catch the ferry from Kamenari across to Lepetane. The country's latest highlight awaits you in ② *Tivat* → p. 45 where enormous luxury yachts float in the water of the Porto Montenegro Marina. From there you can test your driving skills on the winding mountain road and be rewarded with a magnificent view of ③ *Budva* → p. 52 (photo left) bathed in sunlight behind the mountain. Take a leisurely walk through the old part of town with its Venetian houses and then go to one of the nearby beaches for a dip in the sea. You should plan a stopover to at least get a photo of the gem of the Adriatic, the former fishing village on the island of Sveti Stefan. The 12km/7.5mi long beach in ④ *Ulcinj* → p. 61 is not only a fine place for swimming; you can also surf or go horseback riding here.

AROUND LAKE SKADAR

Head to the north via Mount Rumija. A boat from Murići will take you across to make a brief visit to the Orthodox nuns on the island of ⑤ *Beška* → p. 73. After a few meditative moments in the cloister, it's back to the mainland where you will have to exchange four wheels for two: the road to ⑥ *Virpazar* → p. 74 is part of the cycle route around Lake Skadar. When you reach your destination, you will be able to get back your strength with smoked carp or bleak in the Pelikan Restaurant. Another trip by boat brings you to ⑦ *Rijeka Crnojevića* → p. 70. You will glide through the water lilies on the eponymous river as it winds its way picturesquely through the landscape offering endless opportunities for taking lovely photographs.

THE ONLY WAY IS UP

Back on the road, you set off for ⑧ *Tuzi* → p. 28 to go shopping at the largest market in Montenegro. The Morača Canyon starts behind Podgorica, the emerald-green river glitters far down below. Enjoy the peace and tranquillity of the Orthodox ⑨ *Morača Monastery* → p. 89 (photo right) before heading off from ⑩ *Kolašin* → p. 87 to go skiing in the mountains. You can also be active in the Biogradska gora National Park: hiking or exploring nature on horseback

Experience the many facets of Montenegro on a round trip with brief detours to tranquil islands and mountain lakes

or in a Jeep at an altitude of more than 2000m/6560ft.

RIVER COURSES

⓫ *Plav* → p. 89, with its beautiful lake, lies at the foot of the Prokletije Mountains. Only the very brave will attempt a swim – the water is ice-cold. Travel along the Lim River with its gorges to ⓬ *Bijelo Polje* → p. 85, whose churches bear witness to the fact that it was once an important religious centre. Another house of worship awaits you in ⓭ *Pljevlja* → p. 82: the impressive Hussein Pasha Mosque. You reach the second untamed river in Montenegro near Đurđevića Tara. There is a spectacular view down into ⓮ *Tara River Canyon* → p. 83 from a 150m/492ft bridge. From Žabljak you will soon reach the ⓯ *Durmitor National Park* → p. 81, where can spend the night in comfortable huts near the Crno jezero mountain lake.

THE NEW & OLD CAPITAL

A 50-minute train ride takes you from ⓰ *Nikšić* → p. 76 to ⓱ *Podgorica* → p. 70. Shortly before you reach the capital, the oak forests make way for vineyards. The architecture also shows the transition to warmer climes: the houses in the north are squat and made of wood. In the south, you will see typical Mediterranean stone houses. Continue your drive on the road to the old capital ⓲ *Cetinje* → p. 65, where many museums document Montenegro's past. Try the famous smoked ham in Njeguši and then climb the highest peak in the Lovćen Mountains. After you leave the mountains and head towards ⓳ *Kotor* → p. 40, the old road has some wonderful views of the southernmost fjord in Europe. You will be able to admire the palaces built by famous captains in ⓴ *Perast* → p. 44 and then contemplate the good old seafaring days of the city over a meal of grilled scampi. The route then takes you along the Bay of Kotor back to Herceg Novi.

**950km/590mi. Travel time: 23 hours
Recommended duration: 5 days
A detailed map of the route can be
found on the back cover, in the road
atlas and on the pull-out map**

THE BAY OF KOTOR

No matter from where you approach from, the first view of the Bay of Kotor (Boka Kotorska), with its four inlets that cut deep into the mainland, is an unforgettable sight.

Regardless of whether you catch the first glimpse shortly before landing at the airport in Tivat or after driving the serpentine road down from Montenegro's own Olympus, the Lovćen, to Kotor: nowhere else in Montenegro do steep rock walls and the glittering green Adriatic meet as they do here. Harmoniously embedded in this spectacular natural setting are some masterpieces created by man: seen from above, the small church islands off the coast of Perast, Sveti Đorđe and Gospa od Škrpjela (Our Lady of the Rocks), shine in the water like pebbles in a pool. Stretching 28km/17mi into the hinterland the Boka Kotorska – which the Montenegrins simply call Boka – offered seafarers a safe haven from the open waters of the Adriatic. The people living in the area, the *bokelji*, are extremely proud of a history of independence. Due to their sailing prowess, the Kotor fleet, under the flag of the Venetian Republic of Saint Mark, took part in combating the Turkish conquerors. Tsar Peter the Great took on the most famous seamen from the region to train his own captains. A boat tour of the bay provides a vivid

Photo: Kotor

Old ports and 'pearls of nature': rugged mountains frame the heritage of proud seafarers in the only fjord in southern Europe

impression of the unique charm of this southern fjord on through – and you will also be able pay a visit to the church islands off the coast of Perast and the old marine prison Mamula off Herceg Novi.

Its location at at the crossroads between east and west – between Constantinople and Venice, Vienna, Paris and and Moscow – meant that the foreign powers enriched the cosmopolitan spirit of the Boka through

the centuries. The 70km/43mi coast road winds its way past palm trees, small beaches and charming old stone houses from Herceg Novi to Tivat – along with Kotor, the two largest cities on the bay.

A ferry operates between Kamenari and Lepetane on the Verige Strait throughout the year making it possible to travel quickly from the old town of Kotor – with its unique architectural ensemble – to

Steep stairways and paths lead through the old town of Herceg Novi

HERCEG NOVI

MAP INSIDE BACK COVER
(122 C5) (*∅ H5*) ★
The Yugoslavian Nobel Prize laureate Ivo Andrić described Herceg Novi (pop. 14,000) as the city of 'eternal greenery, sun and promenades'.

Herceg Novi, the flower town. Framed by the Orjen Mountains in the west and the Lovćen in the east, the Boka attracted ruling families and sailors from early times and the *bokelji* never really had any peace. When the Roman Empire split in AD 395, the bay became part of the Western Roman Empire while the rest of the Montenegrin coast was ceded to Byzantium. The Venetians left the most significant traces in both the linguistic and culinary fields. Here, you will be served *cappuccino* and *risotto* more often than *ćevapčići* and *pite*.

The English poet Lord Byron visited the Bay of Kotor in 1809 and wrote: 'At the birth of our planet, the most beautiful encounter between the land and the sea must have happened at the coast of Montenegro. When the pearls of nature were sown, handfuls of them were cast on this soil.' His words remain true to this day.

When the north of Montenegro is still in the grip of icy winter temperatures, the first flowers start to bloom in the harbour town that was founded in 1382 by the Bosnian King Tvrtko I and later named after Duke (*Herceg*) Stijepana Vukšić. This is celebrated every year with a feast of wine and fresh fish held in late January/ early February when thousands of people throng the waterfront promenade (*obala*) for the Mimosa Festival.

The city's famous seafarers brought exotic plants with them when they returned from their voyages and, paired with the flora of the Mediterranean region, they blossom in colourful splendour every spring. The mix of architectural styles from Oriental to Baroque lends Herceg Novi – situated on a steep escarpment with long flights of steps – with a touch of elegance that always charms its visitors. The almost 200 days of sun – the most on the Adriatic – does the rest.

The 7km/4mi long promenade *Šetalište Pet Danica* stretches from the spa town of Igalo to Meljine and is lined with cafés, restaurant and jetties. This is the place to see and be seen – with mirror sunglasses, the latest smartphones and designer clothes. The *obala* forms the heart of the Herceg Nova Riviera that stretches from *Njivice* to *Kamenari*. The landmark *Orjen* (1893m/6211ft) dominates the background, the sun rises over the *Prevlaka Peninsula* and sets behind the *Mamula* fortress island built by the Austrian rulers, and there are especially beautiful views of all of this from the *obala*.

The 'City of 100,000 Steps' once again became the favourite holiday destination for Belgrade's artistic elite after the end of the Balkan wars. They are particularly attracted by the cultural activities offered in Herceg Novi. A winter salon opens its doors in the former Benković Gallery in February. Stage performers from the region get together in April for the Theatre Festival and the Herceg Novi Cultural Summer *(www.hercegfest.co.me)* begins in June. The highlight of the series of performances is the classical INSIDER TIP Days of Music in July followed by the Montenegro Film Festival in August.

SIGHTSEEING

GALERIE ●
One of the oldest galleries in the country exhibits modern art by young talents from Serbia and Montenegro. New works by artists from the region are presented and awarded prizes at a winter salon, which has been organised by the collection since 1966. There are plans to rename the gallery, currently dedicated to the freedom fighter and painter Josip Bepo Benković,

---

MARCO POLO HIGHLIGHTS

Popular meeting place in the old town: Trg Nikole Đurkovića, the former 'Salt Square'

but this had not been decided on at the time of going to press. *Daily May–Sept 9am–10pm, Oct–April 9am–7pm | Marka Vojnovića 4 | short.travel/mon7 | free admission*

KANLI KULA

The fortress, which was constructed at the upper end of the old town during the Turkish period, served as a bastion and prison for many years. With seating for more than 1000, it is now one of the most beautiful open air stages on the Adriatic.

STARI GRAD (OLD TOWN)

A flight of steps leads from *Nikole Đurković Square,* the city's bustling meeting place, with cafés and shops, in the centre of town, through Herceg Novi's most famous landmark the clock tower *(Sahat kula)* commissioned by Sultan Mahmud in 1667. The Orthodox Archangel Michael Church *(Sveti Arhanđela Mihaila)*, with its Romanesque, Gothic and Oriental elements, lies behind it on pretty, palm tree fringed *Herceg Stjepan Square*. The city's

archives take up the northern end of the square and there is a library with 30,000 volumes on the south side.

Follow the narrow streets down through the old town and you will land right in front of the entrance to the *Forte Mare.* The fortified tower was constructed between the 14th and 17th century and today films are shown here on a big screen in the summer.

TVRĐAVA ŠPANJOLA (SPANISH FORTRESS)

Construction of this fortress, which towers over the city and offers a magnificent view of the bay and Prevlaka Peninsula, was started by the Spaniards in 1538 and later completed by the Turks.

ZAVIČAJNI MUZEJ

Archaeological finds from the early days of Herceg Novi – when Illyrians, Greeks and Romans settled in the area – are displayed on the two floors of the Regional Museum. A small section of the house is devoted to the Partisan War. *Tue–Sun 9am–8pm |*

Mirka Komnenovića 9 | short.travel/mon8 | entrance fee 2 euros

FOOD & DRINK

Many pizzerias and restaurants serving grilled meat and fish line the *Šetalište Pet Danica*. And, most of the city's beaches are turned into bars, pubs and discotheques in the evening *(information under: www. hercegnovi.travel)*.

BELVEDERE

Enjoy the lovely view of the bay from this restaurant's ☼ terrace while having a delicious fish dinner. Live music is performed every day and guests can use the Wi-Fi free of charge. *Manastirska 2 | mobile 066 952 8140 | www.belvedere-monte negro.me | Moderate–Expensive*

INSIDER TIP KLUB KNJIŽEVNIKA/ KUĆA IVE ANDRIČA

This restaurant is located in the former home of Yugoslavia's Literature Nobel Prize laureate Ivo Andrić. The Nobel Prize certificate and some books are displayed in glass cases. The menu includes fish, seafood and grilled dishes. *Njegoševa 65 | tel. 031 32 17 63 | Moderate*

RAFAELLO

One of the best restaurants in town where the waves almost lap the entrance. Try *crni rižot,* black squid risotto. *Šetalište Pet Danica | tel. 031 32 32 46 | Expensive*

SPORT CAFÉ

Sporting events from around the world are shown on a dozen televisions; the walls are decorated with basketball hoops and posters of Yugoslav sports stars. The meat dishes are sportily listed as the 'Champions League', fish is under 'Sea Stars' and dessert appears as 'Extra Time'. *Šetalište Pet Danica 34 | tel. 031 32 20 18 | Moderate*

SHOPPING

INSIDER TIP SO ●

Opened by book lovers in 2004 the bookstore's name (So means 'salt') is a reminder that Herceg Novi was established in the wake of the salt trade. The premises are located on the former 'Salt Square' where the white gold was traded in times gone by. There is a wide selection of books in many languages and the proprietor is proud to stress that the staff members speak English 'without an accent'. Browse your newly purchased books over a cup of coffee at one of the bars on the square. *Trg Nikole Đurkovića 3 | www.knjizaraso. com*

SPORTS & ACTIVITIES

GORBIS TRAVEL

The travel office not only organises private accommodation but also boat tours of the Bay of Kotor and day trips to Ostrog Monastery near Nikšić, as well as to Dubrovnik and Lake Skadar. *Njegoševa 64 | tel. 031 32 20 85 | www.gorbis.com*

INSIDER TIP PAJO BOAT TOURS

Fish picnics on one of the three boats the owner Dušan Sučević has restored himself are just one of the many highlights of any trip through the Boka. Also on offer are excursions to the beaches on the Luštica Peninsula, to Kotor and Perast, the fortress island of Mamula and the Blue Grotto. Prices range from 10 to 30 euros per person depending on the duration and number of participants. *At the harbour | mobile 067 30 09 69*

TENIS CENTAR SBS

In spring and autumn the site of two Grand Slam Tournaments. Court fees: 7 euros/ hour; under floodlight, 10 euros. Lessons from a trainer cost 15 euros/hour or 18 euros under floodlight. *Šetalište Pet Danica 8a | tel. 031 32 40 40 | www.sbstennis.com*

BEACHES

Herceg Novi's most beautiful beaches, *Žanjice, Mirište, Dobreč* and *Arza,* are on the *Luštica Peninsula (see p. 47)* on the other side of the bay and can be easily reached by boat. The large hotels have manmade beaches (concrete platforms) and there is **INSIDER TIP** a lovely sandy beach *(Blatna plaža)* at the western end of the pedestrian promenade below the Igalo Institute. Boats leave the harbour for *Njivice,* where the nudist beach of the Hotel Riviera is also open to non-guests. Those who prefer to swim further away from town should take the small coastal road towards Bijela where the beaches in *Zelenika, Kumbor, Đenovići* and *Balošići* are not as crowded as those in Herceg Novi. One thing applies here and for all the other beaches in the Bay of Kotor: as there is hardly any inflow from the sea, the water is sometimes becomes a little stagnant.

ENTERTAINMENT

The promenade along the shore stretches for about a mile and is lined with countless bars, cafés, pubs and restaurants. When the heat of the day gives way to the cool of the evening, young and old flock to the beach and have fun there until the early hours of the morning: in the *Bolivar* (local bands), *Casa* (house and techno), *Baron* (three stages), *Nautica* (jazz), *Copas* (with sun loungers on the beach itself).

WHERE TO STAY

Herceg Novi is one of the more expensive locations but there are also some more economical hotels, holiday apartments and private accommodation in the city.

They are usually well equipped and most have Wi-Fi. There is still a great deal of construction activity taking place and it can be noisy in off-season.

INSIDER TIP AURORA
The director Emir Kusturica ('Black Cat, White Cat') bought the venerable Hotel Aurora on the promenade along the shore and tastefully developed it. The boutique hotel has an excellent ● cinema on the ground floor where film classics are shown in the original version. *11 rooms | Šetalište Pet Danica 42 | mobile 069 28 78 65 | aurorahotel.me | Expensive*

ŠKVER ☀
This stone house on a square – hence the name based on the English word – is both a guest house and restaurant. The magnificent complex has a view of the harbour and the rooms are attractively furnished. Good food is served in the restaurant *(Budget). 5 apartments | Šetalište Pet Danica 34 | mobile 069 50 35 56 | skver-apartments.com | Apts. Expensive*

VILA ALEKSANDAR
The pleasant hotel has a spacious terrace and there is a pebble beach directly below the building. *16 rooms | Save Kovačevića 64 | tel. 031 34 58 06 | www.hotel vilaaleksandar.com | Expensive*

INFORMATION

TURISTIČKA ORGANIZACIJA HERCEG NOVI
Jova Dabovića 12 | tel. 031 35 08 20 | www. hercegnovi.travel

WHERE TO GO

BIJELA (123 D5) (*m J5*)
There several smaller villages strung along the Adriatic immediately after Herceg

Novi: *Meljine, Zelenika, Kumbor, Đenovići, Balošići* and *Bijela*. The community (pop. 4000) with its shipyard 14km/9mi from Herceg Novi is the ideal place for divers and other water sports enthusiasts to spend their Boka holiday. The *Hotel Delfin (112 rooms | tel. 031 68 34 00 | www.hotel-delfin.net | Moderate)* has facilities for training, boxing, judo and tennis, football and basketball. The *Regional Center for*

considered to the best restaurant in the country for many years and serves excellent cuisine. Reservations are essential and your meal will cost more than 50 euros per person.

IGALO (122 C5) (*∅ H5*)

This spa town (pop. 3000) at the western end of the waterfront promenade is only a 15-minute walk from the harbour in

The clear water of the Adriatic near Bijela attracts both 'lilo captains' and experienced divers

Divers Training (tel. 031 68 34 77 | www.rcudme.info) organises courses for beginners and advanced divers. The *Villa Azzurro (tel. 031 67 16 06 | www.hotel azzurro.me | Budget)*, with 14 rooms, at the south end of Bijela welcomes its guests to its own beach. In *Morinj*, 8km/5mi towards Kotor, you can dine elegantly in the atmospheric old mill **INSIDER TIP** *Čatovića Mlini (tel. 032 37 30 30 | www.catovicamlini.me | Expensive)*. It has been

Herceg Novi. In the last years of his life, Tito built the Villa Galeb – a luxurious residence with swimming pools and saunas – a little way above the town; today, it is permanently rented to Russian business people. The ● *Institut Igalo* or *Mediterranean Health Center (420 rooms | Save Ilica 1 | tel. 031 65 85 55 | www.igalo spa.com | Moderate)*, which was opened in 1950 to capitalise on the curative qualities of the minerals in the mud from the shore, was extended after Tito's death and now offers every manner of spa treatments including mud packs and galvanic baths (11 euros), aromatherapy (25 euros) and lymph drainage (14 euros).

It is less expensive to stay in one of the numerous private homes or many small hotels scattered throughout the town (information under *www.hercegnovi.travel*). There are also several camping sites on the coast. The *Levanger Restaurant* on the shore side of the *Hotel Tamaris (Obala Nikole Kovačevića 24 | tel. 031 33 21 63 | Moderate)* serves excellent local seafood specialities.

INSIDER TIP ROSE
(122 C6) (*ɯ H6*)

The picturesque village of Rose is on the Luštica Peninsula opposite Herceg Novi. Many Serbian film stars have settled here and it is now known as the 'Saint Tropez of Montenegro'. Roses and oleanders cover the walls of the magnificently renovated stone houses, palm trees provide shade and the beach is on the doorstep. And Herceg Novi, which can be seen from the bedroom windows, is accessible by boat within a few minutes. Tourists can now also rent apartments in Rose; just a few metres away from the sea are the 15 bungalows – for two to four persons – of the *Forte Rose (mobile 067 37 73 11 | www.forterose.me | Expensive)*.

SAVINA (122 C5) (*ɯ H5*)

The small village (pop. 1000) set in lush greenery is only a twenty-minute walk away from the harbour in Herceg Novi. The Orthodox monastery *(daily 7am–7pm | free admission)* with its two churches a little bit above the waterfront promenade has the almost 800-year-old INSIDER TIP Bishop's Cross of Saint Sava, the patron saint of the Serbian Orthodox church, in its treasury.

KOTOR

▓ MAP ON P. 123
(123 E–F 4–5) (*ɯ K5*) **Wake up in the morning to the sound of bells chiming – there are almost a dozen churches in the historic old part of Kotor (pop. 6000). The area was declared a Unesco World Heritage Site after the earthquake in 1979 to ensure that it was reconstructed without delay.**

Every day, the people living in Kotor realise that this has been successful when they relax in one of the cafés on the square – polished smooth by countless footsteps – in front of the clock tower. This is probably the best place to get a feeling for the spirit of the city that was once ruled by the Romans, Venetians and Austrians.

A visit to Kotor means immersing oneself in the Middle Ages when the small town at the south-east corner of the bay was dominated by the Venetians. Kotor is home to the Cathedral of Saint Tryphon built on the foundations of a 9th century church in 1166. Kotor's ancient walls reflect the self-assurance of the independent seafarers' community that always withstood the onslaught of the Turks. It was once named Dekadron and then Catarum, Catera and Cathara by a changing series of rulers. The name of Kotor prevailed among the South Slavs and the Italians turned that into Cattaro. There is a row of picturesque villages along the coast towards Herceg Novi that all have magnificent views of the bay; they are all within easy reach by public bus.

SIGHTSEEING

INSIDER TIP JEWISH CEMETERY
The Jews who came to Montenegro from the Iberian Peninsula in the Middle Ages

were known as 'Spanish Jews'. The new Jewish community in Montenegro has not been able to find any written documents on Jewish life in the country in mediaeval times, but the cemetery in Kotor provides sufficient proof that Jews have lived here for centuries. The cemetery was restored in 2005 and in 2011 when Israel's chief rabbi Yona Metzger visited Montenegro, he placed a small stone on one of the graves as tradition demands. *In the Škaljari district*

POMORSKI MUZEJ
(MARITIME MUSEUM) ●

The three floors of the former palace of the Grgurina family houses an exhibition of sailor's clothing, models of old ships, typical weapons and a relief map of the bay. *15 April–June and Sept–15 Oct Mon–Fri 8am–6pm, Sun 9am–1pm, July–Aug Mon–Fri 8am–11pm, Sun 10am–4pm, 15 Oct–15 April Mon–Fri 9am–5pm, Sat/Sun 9am–noon | Trg Bokeljske mornarice | www.museummaritimum.com | entrance fee 4 euros*

CITY WALLS

Begun in 1420 by the Venetians the city walls, which cut deeply into the mountain above Kotor, were not completed until 400 years later. The walls are more than 4km/2.5mi *(entrance fee 2 euros)* long and the ascent begins a little way behind the north gate. The small *Gospa od Zdravlja* church is located about half way up towards the ☙ *Sveti Ivan* fortress.

STARI GRAD (OLD TOWN) ★ ●

Three gates lead into the historic old town of Kotor; the oldest is the one in the south was built as early as in the 13th century. The northern and main gates *(Morska vrata)* in front of the large car park on the shore – the old town is a pedestrian zone – were built in the Renaissance style in the 16th century. The clock tower *(Sat kula)* can is opposite the main gate with the palaces of the patrician Bisanti and Beskuca families in the background. In addition to the Saint Luka Church, which was shared by Catholic and Orthodox worshipers

This is where you will feel the spirit of this old town: the square in front of the clock tower in Kotor

until well into the 19th century, the Saint Tryphon Cathedral is especially worth visiting. It suffered severe damage in the 1979 earthquake but has since been completely restored.

FOOD & DRINK

BASTION
The restaurant at the northern entrance to the old town offers a splendid range of fresh fish. Try the **INSIDER TIP** squid stuffed with ham and cheese. *Stari grad 517 | tel. 032 32 21 16 | www.bastion123. com | Moderate–Expensive*

GALION ☆
Enjoy the exquisite cuisine of this restaurant right on the waterfront overlooking the old town of Kotor, and choose from between 130 varieties of imported and local wines. *Maceo | tel. 032 32 50 54 | Expensive*

KONOBA CESARICA
Dalmatian fish specialities, but also sheep milk cheese from local farmers and t-bone steaks are on the menu. Near the music school in the old town. *Stari grad 375 | tel. 032 33 60 93 | Expensive*

ENTERTAINMENT

The *Diskoteka Maximus* is located on *Trg oružja* (Weapon Square) and it has all of the trimmings you would expect to find in a trendy disco but things are more peaceful in the piano bar right next door.

WHERE TO STAY

AMFORA ☆
This is one of the new small hotels right on the coast. It is located in *Orahovac,* 8km/ 5mi from Kotor, and also has wonderful views of the majestic mountain backdrop. *12 rooms | tel. 032 30 58 52 | www.amfora-hotel.com | Expensive*

MARIJA
The venerable townhouse in the old town is has a unique interior with beautiful oak panelling. *17 rooms | Stari grad 449 | tel. 032 32 50 62 | www.hotelmarija.me | Expensive*

RENDEZ-VOUS
The Rendez-vous is one of the most reasonably priced establishments in the old town. *10 rooms | Pjaca od mlijeka | tel. 032 32 24 47 | Budget*

VARDAR
An old patrician house – with 33 rooms, Turkish bath and cigar lounge – in the old part of town, surrounded by stone houses.

LOW BUDGET

▶ The small but elegant family-run guest house, the *Arnaut (14 rooms | Njegoševa 111 | mobile 067 30 73 23 | www.pansionarnaut.net)* in Herceg Novi, has extremely reasonable rates for the area. In August, a double room only costs 13 euros and this drops to 10 euros in the off season. Prices are negotiable from October to May. The guest house is only three minutes away from the pedestrian precinct and a 20m/66ft from the beach and there are even tennis courts in the immediate vicinity.

▶ *La Pasteria (Pjaca Sveti Tripun | tel. 032 32 22 69)* in Kotor offers 'honest Italian food': prices for pizza and pasta start at 5 euros and the view of the cathedral is included free of charge.

The magnificently decorated interior of the Gospa od Škrpjela

Ask for ✨ INSIDER TIP room 206 as Kotor's elegant promenade is right below its balcony. *Stari grad 476 | tel. 032 32 50 84 | www.hotelvardar.com | Expensive*

INFORMATION

TURISTIČKA ORGANIZACIJA KOTORA
Stari grad 315 | tel. 032 32 28 86 | www. kotor.travel

WHERE TO GO

DOBROTA (123 E4) *(⨑ K4–5)*
This suburb of Kotor (pop. 7000) has many small beaches and stretches for more than 7km/4mi along the coast. The *Ellas Restaurant (mobile 069 24 43 42 | Budget–Moderate)* on the waterfront offers something a little different as it specialises in Greek food. There are simple multi-bed rooms in the *Dobrotski Dvori* guesthouse *(8 rooms | tel. 032 33 08 40 | Budget)*, also on the coast. If you want to

spend the night in more elegant surroundings then you should book into the *Palazzo Radomiri (tel. 032 33 31 72 | www.palazzoradomiri.com | Expensive)*. A Russian Montenegrin family has developed the 18th century Baroque palace and each of the seven rooms has been named after the ships that once belonged to the Rasomiri family. Although it is directly on the waterfront, it also has a swimming pool.

GOSPA OD ŠKRPJELA ★
(123 D4) *(⨑ J4)*
One of the highlights of any Boka trip is a visit to the two church islands off the coast near Perast. The original Gospa od Škrpjela (Our Lady of the Rocks) was built in 1452. Every year, boats sail across on 22 July to celebrate the anniversary by throwing stones into the water around the island. This custom has a long tradition: for decades, sailors and fishermen sunk boats and piled up boulders on what

was originally the small area of the rock until, in the middle of the 17th century, there was enough space to expand the church and add some new buildings. The house of worship was given its Baroque interior by the architect Ilija Katičić who added the bell tower and improved the nave of the church.

The paintings on the walls and ceiling were created by the famous artist Tripo Kokolja (1661–1713), whose work was extremely popular in the Adriatic region from Dubrovnik to Venice. The hundreds of votive pictures in the church showing ships and scenes of everyday life in Perast are are tokens of appreciation for being healed of a disease.

The island *Sveti Đorđe* (Saint George), opposite Gospa od Škrpjela, was for a long period the most important Benedictine abbey in the bay. In contrast to its sister church, Sveti Đorđe dominates the scene from atop a natural stone reef. Boat tours can be booked in all of the towns and villages on the coast.

PERAST ★
(123 D–E4) *(Ø J4)*

This attractive town boasts the most hours of sunshine per day in the country. The busts in front of the 15th century Baroque *Sveti Nikola* church, with its 55m/180ft high bell tower, indicate what the town is famous for: its captains, who also taught Tsar Peter the Great's sailors all they knew. Today, only 300 people live in the village – which is a protected area – but, at one time, the fleet of this community (that was declared autonomous in 1558) was larger than that of Dubrovnik.

Perast is around 14km/9mi from Kotor and is one of the most beautiful small Baroque towns on the Adriatic. Under Venetian rule for centuries, it was repeatedly attacked by the ships of the Ottoman Empire but they were never able to take the city. Its status as an important border town gave its inhabitants many privileges that ended abruptly with the fall of Venice in 1797 and led to the downfall of the proud fraternity of seamen. The *Museum (May–*

The beautiful little Baroque town of Perast was once a stronghold of proud seafarers

June and Sept Mon–Sat 9am–5pm, Sun 9am–2pm, July–Aug 9am–7pm, Sun 9am–2pm, Oct–April daily 8am–2pm | on the shore | www.muzejperast.me | entrance fee 2.50 euros) in Perast is located in the *Bujović Palace* from the 17th century. Portraits of the city's illustrious captains, maps and the furnishings of the Bujović's make it possible for visitors to immerse themselves in the bygone world of the seafarers. The **INSIDERTIP** *Hotel Conte (10 apartments | Obala Kapetana Marka Martinovića | tel. 032 37 36 87 | www.hotel-conte.com | Moderate)* was also once a captain's house. The restaurant *(Moderate)* is right on the sea and you simply must try the grilled scampi.

PRČANJ (123 E4) (*M K4*)

Prčanj (pop. 1000) is around 6km/4mi from Kotor on the bay. The town's seamen established the first postal service between Venice and Constantinople in the 17th century. There is a monument to Prčanj's most famous captain, Ivo Visin, in front of the parish church *Bogordični hram*, the largest in the Boka. The **INSIDERTIP** *Splendido Hotel (43 rooms | Naselje Glavati | tel. 032 30 17 00 | www.splendido-hotel. com | Expensive)*, with swimming pool and direct access to the sea, is named after the ship Visin used for his circumnavigation of the world.

RISAN (123 D3–4) (*M J4*)

The Illyrian Queen Teuta established her residence in the oldest town on the bay (pop. 1500), which is around 18km/11mi from Kotor, in the 3rd century BC before being taken by the Romans about 100 years later. The mosaic floors from the Roman period, when Risan was the most important town in the region, can be seen in an unguarded *open air museum (always open | free admission)* a short way above the filling station.

TIVAT

(123 E5) (*M J–K5*) **Tivat (pop. 11,500) was a sleepy place that mainly served as a base for military ships for many years.** The Venetians controlled the city until 1797, followed by the Austro-Hungarian Empire that took advantage of Tivat's strategic location at the entrance to the bay to develop a naval base there. Warships were still anchored in Tivat in the 20th century: the town was the most important military base in the southern Adriatic in Tito's era. The well-established marine arsenal re-equipped Yugoslavian and Soviet warships during the Cold War period. Tivat and its airport were closed to tourism for many years. It was not until the second half of the 20th century that the city slowly opened up but it remained more a place people passed through than stopped in to spend their holiday. In 2006, the Canadian billionaire Peter Munk bought the run-down shipyards for three million dollars, took a ninety-year lease on the adjacent property and promised to build Europe's best marina in Tivat. No sooner said than done – today ★ *Porto Montenegro (www. portomontenegro.com)* has 630 moorings and enormous yachts have their home port here. With his investment, Munk managed to do something many other foreign investors failed at: he was able to awaken this 'sleeping beauty'. Since then the town has developed into one of the region's main tourism centres.

Next to the marina a Mediterranean town – with luxurious apartments, narrow and winding streets, taverns, and ● fashion boutiques from the likes of Gaultier and Stella McCartney – has emerged on the waterfront. Those who do not want to spend the night on their luxury yachts can sleep in their own home on the dry land after paying as much as 10,000 euros per square metre for the privilege. The new Hotel Regent Porto Montenegro will open its doors in 2014 but it is worth visiting Porto Montenegro even if you do not spend the night in opulent lodgings: you can feast and sip champagne on the waterside in *One (mobile 067 48 60 45 | Expensive)* or plunge into the 64m/210ft pool with spectacular views across the Bay of Kotor in the ● *Purobeach (20 euros/day | www. purobeach.com)* temple of relaxation.

SIGHTSEEING

YUGOSLAVIAN GENERAL CONSULATE

Yugoslavia has become history but the state still has a general consulate in Tivat. The telephone number is identical to the founding date of the Socialist republic (29.11.43). There are all kinds of devotional objects such as flags, badges and old postcards on display. And, if you want to, you can be issued with a 'genuine' Yugoslavian passport for a mere 10 euros. *Daily 10am–5pm | Palih Borača 4 | free admission*

MUZEJ I GALERIJA LJETNIKOVCA BUĆA

The Buca family's former summer residence dates back to 1548 and now houses a cultural centre with a small town museum displaying photos of Tivat from the 19th and early 20th centuries. *Daily 7am–11pm | behind the harbour | free admission*

FOOD & DRINK

BACCHUS

This restaurant is a little bit away from the others on the waterfront promenade and is very popular with the locals. You should try the delicious squid stuffed with shrimps! *Palih Borača | tel. 032 67 25 58 | Moderate*

MONTENEGRINO

The Montenegrino is the top restaurant in town. Gourmets will relish the lobster.

21. Novembra 27 | tel. 032 67 49 00 | Expensive

INSIDER TIP ▶ PROVA

From the outside, the Prova looks like a ship on dry land under palm trees. It is possible to spend the entire day on one of the comfy rattan sofas: breakfast is served in the morning and there is a top-rate dinner in the evening. The restaurant serves Mediterranean cuisine at inexpensive prices. *Šetalište Iva Vizina 1 | tel. 032 67 14 68 | www.prova.co.me | Budget*

BEACHES

The *Oblatno Bay* with its exclusive beach is only a short distance away from Tivat: the complex not only provides the standard sun loungers (3 euros a day) but also a so-called 'living room'. Those who are prepared to pay 50 euros (a day) will have a sofa, chairs and plasma TV at their disposal under the shade of a white canopy. The *Plavi horizonti* beach on the other side of Tivat is just as close and has also been awarded the Blue Flag.

WHERE TO STAY

PALMA ⛅

This is the best preserved of the three old state-run hotels, with a splendid view of the Adriatic. *114 rooms | Pakovo | tel. 032 67 22 88 | www.primorje.me | Moderate*

PINE ⛅

People who stay here have a direct view of the pedestrian promenade at the harbour. *26 rooms | tel. 032 67 13 05 | htpmimoza.me | Moderate*

VILLA ROYAL

The attractive new building is located behind the marina. *6 rooms, 6 apartments | Kalimanj | tel. 032 67 53 10 | Expensive*

Olive trees have been cultivated on the Luštica Peninsula since antiquity

INFORMATION

TURISTIČKA ORGANIZACIJA TIVAT
Palih Borača 8 | tel. 032 671323 | www. tivat.travel

WHERE TO GO

LUŠTICA ★
(122–123 C–E 5–6) *(ⓜ H–J 5–6)*

The Montenegrins call this 18 square mile peninsula just south of Tivat the 'Land of Olives'. Almost every bay on Luštica has a beach. Olive trees have grown here since ancient times and most of the houses used to have their own olive mills; the people here lived with – and from – olives. Later Luštica came under the control of the military that guarded the entrance to the Bay of Kotor from here. Many residents departed but now their grandchildren are returning and they are not the only ones who feel at home here: the Mayor of Moscow has a residence and a Russian village has developed in the hills. There are plans to follow all this with new villas, hotels and a super marina. The 35km/22mi long coastline is still fairly empty and the unspoiled bays with their turquoise water lie in secluded in the sun. The interior of Luštica is also charming: deserted villages, stone houses in the shade of olive groves, and all of that in clear, fresh air; *Obosnik* Mountain is 582m/1910ft high. *Plava Špilja*, the Blue Grotto, is on the south side of the island.

PREVLAKA (123 E5) *(ⓜ K5)*
The abundance of plant life on Prevlaka has earned it the name *Ostrvo cvijeća* which means Flower Island; it can be reached by boat from Tivat.

THE ADRIATIC

Beaches stretching for miles and picturesque bays, small sections of sandy coast hidden between the rocks and a green hinterland that almost reaches the shore. This is Montenegro's Adriatic coast.

The peaks of the Lovćen and Rumija soar up into the sky behind the delightful little harbour towns on the coast and offer tourists travelling from Podgorica or Cetinje majestic views from the heights. A picturesque landscape stretches from Budva to the island of Ada Bojana just before the Albanian border: small fishing boats rocked gently by the waves, countless olive groves hidden in the beautiful hills, stone houses from another era and avenues lined with pine trees and cypresses. The Montenegrin Adriatic remained undiscovered as a tourist destination for many years. There were only two hotels in Budva before the Second World War. In the 1960s construction was begun on the coast road – the Jadranska magistrala, that runs from Bar to Rijeka in northern Croatia – and ushered in a new era. Hotels sprung up in next to no time. Private tour companies flew their customers to Dubrovnik and they could reach their accommodation after a short bus ride. The then tiny airport at Podgorica was also expanded. Flocks of tourists – mainly from Germany, Austria and Switzerland – flowed into the country. All of a sudden, German

Photo: The old town of Budva

Magnificent scenery on the Montenegrin Riviera: long beaches and picturesque towns surrounded by green hills

was spoken in Montenegro – the waiters and maids took crash courses to learn a smattering of the language. Ulcinj, which seemed to be at the end of the world next to the border to Albania, became a destination for tourists from the German Democratic Republic. They spent their holidays there in large groups, watched over and strictly segregated from holidaymakers from West Germany. One highlight of the trip was a coach excursion to Dubrovnik – not all East Germans made it back to their hotel; many took the opportunity to escape to the West.

The second wave of construction began after the 1979 earthquake. The people living on the coast in particular were given favourable loans to renovate and make alterations to the houses. The first *vikendice*, weekend cottages, were built.

A holiday on Montenegro's Adriatic coast: beach, sea and a historic backdrop – here, in Budva

Today, the Montenegrin Adriatic is a real gem in spite of the congested roads and water shortages in summer. The architectural traces in Budva, Stari Bar and the old town in Ulcinj left by foreign conquerors – Illyrians, Romans, Venetians and Austrians occupied and defended the harbour towns for centuries – are even more enchanting than in most other parts of Montenegro. The border between the Byzantine and Roman Empires ran south of Budva and the Ottomans repeatedly contested the bastions of the country's Christian rulers.

There are hidden bays and coves between the three main destinations on the Adriatic, Budva, Petrovac and Ulcinj, and tourist agencies organise fish picnics in many places – change your perspective and enjoy the view of the beaches and small towns on the Montenegrin Riviera from a boat. The Sozina Tunnel *(2.50 euros)* has shortened the travel time from the interior of the country to the coast near Sutomore by many miles and scores of visitors from Podgorica use it in summer. However,

tourists from abroad will find the winding ● road from Virpazar near Petrovac more interesting. It runs through a unique area: on one side a lunar landscape and on the other breathtaking views of the sea. And, you will also save on the tunnel toll.

BAR

(126 A–B 4–5) *(M P7)* The city has developed rapidly in recent decades. Bar (pop. 15,000) now has a network of wide streets and boulevards. Construction is everywhere and there are high-rise buildings and shopping malls shooting up all over.

Bar's population is young – courses at the faculties of journalism and business administration are sought after by students from all parts of Montenegro. The city is also increasingly becoming the cultural and economic centre of the southern Adriatic. The marina has moorings for 900 vessels, the harbour is abuzz with activity. The permanent ferry connections to Bari and Ancona, as well as the railroad from Belgrade, bring tourists into the city. Although many do not stay very long, Bar still profits from them.

SIGHTSEEING

GRADSKI MUZEJ (CITY MUSEUM)

Artefacts from many centuries are on display in the former summer residence of King Nikola on the waterfront promenade. *Daily 9am–1pm | Obala 13. Jula | entrance fee 1 euro*

FOOD & DRINK

The best tip is to head to the harbour where you will find a slew of restaurants in various price categories on the promenade. The views of the sailing boats are included in the price of the meal. The *Restoran Savoia (Jovana Tomaševića 16 | mobile 069 63 33 33 | www.restoransavoia.me | Budget–Moderate)* near the farmers' market has a wide selection of pizza and pasta, as well as fish and meat dishes, on its menu.

SHOPPING

The large supermarkets in the centre of Bar offer excellent possibilities for shopping (and they are also the cheapest in the region). On no account should you miss the INSIDER TIP *farmers' market (7am–2pm | Bar pijaca)*, which is also held in the city centre. Vast quantities of fruit and vegetables, fresh fish, heavy hams, honey and olive oil, bay leaves and rosemary, every possible kind of goat's cheese – the market offers a colourful selection of all the region's produce and the aroma is heavenly!

INFORMATION

TURISTIČKA ORGANIZACIJA BAR

Obala 13. Jula | tel. 030 311 6 23 | www.bar.travel

MARCO POLO HIGHLIGHTS

★ Stari Bar
The ruins at the foot of Mount Rumija are all that remain of Stari Bar → p. 52

★ Stari Grad (old town) in Budva
The centuries-old heritage of the Venetians stands proudly between stone walls on a small peninsula → p. 53

★ Sveti Stefan
The most beautiful photo opportunity in the country and a meeting place for the rich, the famous and the beautiful: what was once a fishermen's island has been transformed into a luxurious hotel → p. 56

★ Petrovac na Moru
Old houses on the promenade and palm trees on the beach: the small coastal village has managed to retain much of its charm → p. 57

★ Buljarica
Unimpaired views of the beach and sea from the pristine land behind the beach where the ground is too wet to support development → p. 60

★ Velika plaža (Grand Beach) in Ulcinj
The longest beach in Montenegro is very popular with both children and surfers: the former love the shallow water; the later, the strong winds → p. 62

Close to each other but separated by centuries: the bell tower and Sveti Ivan in Budva

WHERE TO GO

DOBRA VODA AND UTJEHA
(126 C5) (⊞ P–Q 7–8)

You will be well rewarded if you head towards Ulcinj and decide to stay at one of these two bays around 10–15km/6–9mi past Bar. There are very inexpensive holiday apartments and rooms, the sea is on the doorstep, cypresses and pine trees surround the area and the chirping of the crickets is thrown in for free. It is particularly lovely here in May when the ● broom is in full blossom and the region is a sea of yellow. *Ani Apartmani (mobile 069 02 76 86 | www.ani-apartmani.com | Budget)* rents 14 holiday apartments in Dobra Voda. Some of the bungalows in *President Utjeha (8 apartments, 4 bungalows | mobile 069 44 93 93 | www.presidentutjeha.com | Moderate)* are set in an olive grove.

STARI BAR ★ (126 B4) (⊞ P7)

Old *(stari)*, historic Bar is located about 4km/2.5mi north of Bar and 18km/11mi from Ulcinj at the ascent to Mount Rumija. The origins of the city, which is surrounded by a mighty wall, can be traced back to the 11th century when Bar was part of the Serbian coastal state of Zeta. The city gate, whose façade was reconstructed in the 14th century, also dates from this period. St George's Cathedral was erected in the Romanesque Gothic style in the 12th century. The remains of an even older church have been discovered beneath its walls. There are also traces of the time the Turks occupied the city; one of the buildings from this period is the old hammam. *June–Oct open all day | entrance fee 1 euro*

BUDVA

▚▚▚ MAP INSIDE BACK COVER
▚▚▚ (124 C5–6) (⊞ L–M6) **No matter whether you drive down from Cetinje or arrive from Tivat, the first impression of the oldest city (pop. 10,000) on the Montenegrin coast is really spectacular.**

The historic heart of the city lies on a peninsula in the Adriatic a short distance away from the rest of the coast and stretches towards the island of *Sveti Nikola*. The Venetians gave the old town its magnificent appearance in the 15th century; Budva was only slightly damaged in the earthquake in 1979 and any traces of this have long disappeared.

No community in Montenegro has grown as quickly as Budva. The sell-out of property started immediately after the Balkan wars and today even the neighbouring mountains have been built on and integrated into the city. There are real estate offices, as well as villas and apartments, on every corner. Living in the mountains with a pool and sea view is now all the rage because the city is often overcrowded – especially in summer. There is an acute lack of parking space, the roads around the town are jammed and water is short in the high season. But Budva has still remained a magnet that particularly draws in Serbs and Russians: the city with the most beautiful girls, the flashiest cars and highest prices on the coast also boasts the longest nights in the discos, good food on the *obala* and designer fashion in the old town.

SIGHTSEEING

CITADELA (CITADEL)

The old fortress in front of the main square in the old section of town serves as an open air theatre in summer. A few models of old ships – including Columbus' 'Santa Maria' – are on display inside.

MUZEJ GRADA BUDVE

The city museum, possibly the most beautiful in the country, was recently renovated and has many exhibits from Budva's long history dating back to the 5th century BC. Clay bowls and jugs, metal tools and coins from the Roman period are displayed in the house in the old town and give an excellent overview of the past of what was once an Illyrian settlement. *Daily 9am–midnight | Petrovića 11 | entrance fee 2 euros*

STARI GRAD (OLD TOWN) ★

Although the city's rulers changed frequently, architects from Venice made the strongest impact on the appearance of the pretty old town: they conquered Budva in 1442, built many churches as well as the still well-preserved city wall, which they constructed on top of remains of an ancient wall. The 9th century triple-nave Church of Saint John the Baptist *(Sveti Ivan) and* the bell tower *(Sahat kula)*, which was erected in 1867, are also well worth seeing.

FOOD & DRINK

CHICKEN RESTAURANT

The name of this low-priced restaurant says it all: located at the entrance to the old town, the chicken dishes it serves make a welcome change from the pizza and fish that dominates the cuisine in Budva. *Vuka Karadžića 1 | tel. 033 45 13 14 | Budget*

JADRAN – KOD KRSTA

This fish restaurant right at the harbour caters to all tastes: in addition to seafood, fresh fish and lobster, the menu lists typical Montenegrin meat dishes as well as **INSIDER TIP** reasonably priced set meals of the day. *Slovenska obala 10 | tel. 086 45 10 28 | Budget–Moderate*

INSIDER TIP KANGAROO

The restaurant, whose owner also runs a hotel *(24 rooms | Moderate)*, is located in New Budva on the coast road that cuts through Budva. It has a large terrace and a fine selection of well-prepared, inexpensive fish and meat dishes on the menu. *Jadranski put | tel. 033 45 86 53 | www.kangaroo.co.me | Budget–Moderate*

KONOBA KNEZ

You can see the chef at work in the small restaurant and choose the fish you want to eat yourself. *Stjepan M. Lubiša 5 | mobile 069 47 50 25 | Moderate*

O SOLE MIO

Omelettes in the morning, tasty pizzas and pasta for lunch or in the evening – and you can enjoy it all with a view of Budva's bustling waterfront promenade. *Slovenska obala 15 | tel. 033 40 37 20 | Budget*

LEISURE & SPORT

Sports fans will find everything they could possibly wish for on almost every corner and especially at the *Slovenska plaža* beach: bungee jumping, jet skiing, diving, snorkelling and surfing. A real must that only costs around 30 euros is an **INSIDER TIP** all-day excursion with the high-speed boat to Dubrovnik in Croatia. The small boats ply past the beaches and small towns on the Riviera several times a day. The tracks of the **INSIDER TIP** miniature railroad, which connects Budva with the drowsy hamlet of *Rafajlovići* until late in the night, run almost right along the beach.

BEACHES

JAZ

The long pebble beach at Jaz is only around 3km/2mi from Budva towards Tivat. There is a camping site and a few beach bars but no hotels. The rock concerts held at Jaz are legendary: the Rolling Stones and Madonna have both performed here!

MOGREN I AND II

The two beaches, separated from each other by a steep rock face, are only a few minutes away from the Hotel Avala and are much more peaceful than the town beach and Slovenska plaža. A handful of cafés and pubs serve refreshments and it is also possible to hire pedal boats here.

SLOVENSKA PLAŽA

The long shingle beach stretches for a few hundred feet from the harbour to the end of the bay at Budva in the direction of Bečići. There is no lack of pubs here and there is even the possibility to go bungee jumping.

ENTERTAINMENT

Budva is one large nightclub. The Montenegrins love loud music and it booms out of each and every beach bar until late at night. Most of the clubs can be found along *Slovenska obala*.

WHERE TO STAY

The choice of hotels in Budva is one of the best in the whole country but it is a good idea – especially in the high season in July and August – to look for a place to stay in one of the smaller towns in the vicinity or fall back on private accommodation to avoid the crowds.

AVALA ᠅

The old Grand Hotel Avala was torn down and replaced by a new one with all the trimmings. The swimming pool is directly above the beach and the view of the bay and walls of the old town is impressive. But beware: the booming bass from the hotel discotheque can be heard and felt until late at night in some of the rooms. *290 rooms | Mediteranska 2 | tel. 033 40 26 56 | www.avalaresort.com | Expensive*

INSIDER TIP ▶ **VILA LUX**

This well cared for house is conveniently located on the road towards Tivat. Those who are not discouraged by the quarter hour walk to the old part of town will be rewarded with excellent value for money. *22 rooms | Jadranski put | tel. 033 45 59 51 | www.vilalux.com | Moderate*

INFORMATION

TURISTIČKA ORGANIZACIJA BUDVA
Mediteranska 4 | tel. 033 40 28 14 | www. budva.travel

WHERE TO GO

BEČIĆI
(124 C5) *(ᗰ M6)*

To this day the residents of this coastal village (pop. 2000) are still proud that their 2km/1mi of beach was voted the most beautiful in the Mediterranean in Paris in 1936. Foreign investors have built luxurious four and five star hotels overlooking Bečići Beach (just under 2km/1mi from the centre of Budva). Spas and relaxation, caviar and lobster are all on the agenda there. The *Hotel Splendid* not only has suites that cost 1000 euros a night but also its own helicopter landing sites. Several travel organisations offer stays in these magnificent buildings at affordable prices. The hotels *Splendid, Montenegro* and *Blue Star* are run by the *Montenegro-stars Hotel Group (tel. 033 77 37 77 | www. montenegrostars.com*. Tourists who can do without a lift that takes them straight from their room down to the sandy beach should consider staying in one of the much more reasonably-priced private holiday apartments in Bečići. *Stella di Mare (32 rooms | mobile 069 02 66 46 | www.stella-di-mare-apartments.com | Moderate)* on the other side of the coast road, is a few hundred feet from the beach and offers all amenities including cable TV, air conditioning and a terrace.

Just outside of Budva is the 2km/1mi long sandy beach of the small coastal village of Bečići

PRŽNO (124 C6) (〽 M6)

It is also possible to spend wonderful sunny days in the appealing Bay of Pržno 3km/2mi further down the road along the coast towards Petrovac and Ulcinj. A couple of *konobas* at the eastern end of the beach invite visitors to stay a while. The ● *Maestral (171 rooms | tel. 033 41*

complex one of the best in the world once again. At the time this guide went to press, there were speculations in the media that a new sale was about to take place – it seems that the island's future is uncertain.

The island was inaccessible for five years before Victor Restis took it over; the

One of the most photographed sites in Montenegro: the former fishing island of Sveti Stefan

0109 | www.maestral.info | Expensive) has one of the many hotel casinos that are especially popular with weekend tourists from Italy.

SVETI STEFAN ★
(124 C6) (〽 M6)

Opinions are divided: some say that Montenegro has sold its soul, others feel that it is positive and think that the sale of the small island (9km/6mi from Budva) to the Greek shipping magnate Victor Restis will finally make the hotel

Singaporean investors who owned it before him kept a low profile and didn't spend any money on their property. The small enchanted island with its red-roofed stone houses – that is connected to the mainland via a narrow causeway – remained merely the most photographed subject in Montenegro. The ☀ view of the 'Pearl of the Adriatic' from the main road has certainly been captured millions of times.

Sveti Stefan served as a holiday destination for the well heeled for many years after the local fishermen were removed from their small island in 1956. From the outside, it appeared that the compact village had remained unchanged since the 15th century. However, the interiors of the stone houses had been converted into the epitome of luxury. The approximately 100 buildings were turned into holiday villas and the 4 acre island became the most expensive hotel in what was then Yugoslavia in 1960. The list of VIPs who have stayed there is long – Orson Welles, Elizabeth Taylor, Claudia Schiffer and Silvester Stallone, Sophia Loren and Princess Margaret, and many others.

After Victor Restis took over the island it was carefully and luxuriously renovated and reopened as the *Aman Sveti Stefan* (tel. 033 42 00 00 | www.amanresorts.com | *Expensive*). Its prices may be steep but the Sveti Stefan is regularly booked out. Miločer, the former summer residence of the Yugoslavian kings, which was built in the 1930s, is also part of the complex.

Those who prefer to admire the view of Sveti Stefan in peace from the outside can make themselves comfortable on the beach on the promontory – provided they are prepared to pay around 100 euros for two sun loungers!

PETROVAC NA MORU

(125 D6) (*ØØ N6*) ★ **The tranquil little town (pop. 5000) in a small bay lies directly beneath the coastal road that leads from Sveti Stefan to Bar.**

The settlement originally only consisted of a series of Venetian houses right on the bay – as *na moru* means 'on the sea'. The promenade has remained beautiful thanks to these houses that have been there for centuries. The forefathers of the inhabitants of Petrovac, who are members of the powerful Paštrovići clan, came down from the mountains above today's coast road where some of their stone houses have been preserved to this day.

Although there are many villas, apartments and small hotels in Petrovac, its location between the road and sea has to a large extent prevented the town from falling victim to the country's construction craze. Steps lead down to the water from the Medinski krš district shortening the distance to the town beach. However, it is much more pleasant to wander through the small alleys and breathe in the perfume of the Mediterranean plants as you

OLIVES

More than 100,000 olive trees grow on the slopes and hills around Bar alone; most of them on the way to Ulcinj. One of the oldest trees – believed to be 2000 years old – is in the small village of *Mirovica*, just before Stari Bar. Ulcinj's famous cold-pressed oil is still made in the traditional way: huge cylindrical millstones grind the fruit until all of the bitterness has been pressed out. The oil is then stored for several weeks in various water basins and garlic is added at frequent intervals. Here, as in Tunisia or on the Côte d'Azur, locals believe that the regular consumption of the oil guarantees a long and healthy life.

do. There are palm trees and cypresses at the beach and cafés, pubs and restaurants wait to welcome their guests not even 30m away. The *Café Cuba (Obala | mobile 069 03 43 63)*, which is decorated with pictures of Che and Castro in the interior, is a good place to relax and sip a Mojito or latte macchiato. You can settle down on one of the ● old benches under the trees next to the beach – a pleasant alternative to the sun loungers on the beach itself that cost 10 euros a day. And, you will still have the same view of the sea.

The two small monasteries in the town (14th and 15th century) are beautifully illuminated at night. There is a church on the island of *Sveta Neđelja* just off the coast; it is said that a sailor built it out of gratitude for having been rescued from the sea. There are daily boat excursions to the island.

As is the case with many other towns on the coast, Petrovac is also overcrowded during the high season. It is much more beautiful – and much less expensive – here in May and June when the flowering broom bushes cover the area in a sea of yellow, or in September when the water is almost lukewarm.

SIGHTSEEING

KASTEL LASTVA

The town was named after the fortress on the western edge of the Petrovac Bay up until the end of the First World War.

FOOD & DRINK

CASTIO

Dana Đukovič-Kučko, a real Paštrović, learned all there is to know about cooking and serving in while working in a top hotel abroad. She returned to Petrovac almost 30 years ago, opened her gourmet restaurant with only six tables on the promenade and named it after the old name of the town. She specialises in all kinds of fish and seafood. *Obala | tel. 033 46 11 32 | Moderate–Expensive*

FORTUNA

What makes this restaurant, and the others on the *obala* (the waterfront promenade), so special is not only the excellent food but also the 'roof' of leaves of the rubber plants that flourish in the garden. There are also sea views. The first-rate fillet steak and pasta are highly recommended. *Obala | mobile 069 65 50 00 | Budget–Moderate*

LAZARET

This restaurant next to the fortress on the promenade not only provides internet access but also serves the best pizza in Petrovac. *Obala | mobile 069 02 61 57 | Moderate*

INSIDER TIP ▶ LESKOVAČKI ĆEVAP

Ćevap is the general term for grilled Balkan specialities and Leskovac is a city in southern Serbia that is famous for its *ćevapčići* (rolls of minced meat), *pljeskavica* (hamburgers) and *ražnjići* (grilled skewers of meat). A master griller from Leskovac comes to Petrovac every summer to serve his guests excellent dishes, prepared right before their eyes. It is easy to find the restaurant; just follow your nose along the promenade. *Obala | Budget*

BEACHES

INSIDER TIP ▶ LUĆICE

This shingle beach (about 250m/820ft long and 30m/100ft wide) is surrounded by two lovely, high green slopes and is just past the Hotel Rivijera on the way out of Petrovac.

WHERE TO STAY

PALAS

Large tour operators used to put up their package-deal clients here in the 1970s and it is hoped that things will be the same in the years to come. Spacious rooms with balconies and a swimming pool only separated from the sea by the coast road. *171*

INSIDER TIP ▶ RIVIJERA

One of the most beautiful hotels in Montenegro lies tucked away at the eastern end of the bay: spacious rooms with modern furnishings and a lot of greenery make it easy for the guests to really relax. And, the beach is only 50m/165ft away. *49 rooms | Obala | tel. 033 42 21 00 | www. hotel-rivijera-montenegro.com | Expensive*

The idyllic little town of Petrovac na Moru stretches down the mountain to a small bay

rooms | Obala | tel. 033 42 11 00 | Budget– Moderate

HOTEL PETROVAC

The five-storey building is tastefully furnished and only a five-minute walk away from the beach, bank and supermarkets. The prices are reasonable even in high season. *17 rooms | Medinski krš | tel. 033 46 18 32 | www.hotelpetrovac.me | Moderate*

INSIDER TIP ▶ VUKSANOVIĆ APARTMENTS

One special feature of this establishment is the friendly and helpful proprietors, Branka and Dragan. The five holiday apartments of different sizes – up to three rooms – are all well equipped, there are sea views from some of the terraces and barbecue facilities in the garden, as well as Wi-Fi and cable TV. *5 apartments | Medinski krš | tel. 033 46 18 79 | www. montenegro.ch | Moderate–Expensive*

BULJARICA ⭐

(125 E6) (*ℳ N6*)

2km/1mi south of Petrovac, this long stretch of bay is free of hotels – a rarity in Montenegro. The subterranean springs have prevented the development of Buljarica as it would be much too expensive to drain the ground. So the mile long beach gleams in the sunshine in all of its pristine glory. The eponymous village is located below the coastal road and is surrounded by lush greenery. Tourists who stay here have a ten minute walk to the beach but this is compensated for by the friendly staff and low prices. One such example, *Studio Apartmani Đuković (mobile 069 81 00 03 | Moderate)* offers four inexpensive holiday apartments. The camping site *Camping Maslina (tel. 033*

46 12 15 | akmaslina@t-com.me), is located in an olive grove near the sea. There are a few pubs and small guest houses right next to the water. Health is the top priority at the ● INSIDER TIP *Savojo Hotel (4 rooms, 4 apartments | tel. 033 46 18 76 | www.hotelsavojo.com | Moderate–Expensive)*, also right on the coast: the owner is a practitioner of sports medicine, his son a chiropractor and both offer physiotherapy programmes by the beach. They also serve organic products and wine from their own cellar. The winds across the water change every hour and also contribute to one's physical wellbeing – they are great for the lungs!

SUTOMORE

(126 A4) (*ℳ O7*)

The name of the town (pop. 2000, 13km/8mi from Petrovac) can be traced back to the Italian *sotto mare* and means 'the lower sea'. The long sandy beach remained unspoiled by tourism until two hotels opened their doors in the 1960s; most of the guests at the time were package holiday tourists who were not very demanding. The wind and water were sufficient to make them forget the shortcomings of the Socialist concrete buildings. Today Sutomore has countless reasonably-priced accommodation options; there are small hotels and apartment houses all the way up to the coast road. However, you will only find peace and quiet higher up the mountain – as so often in Montenegro, the beach turns into a one long disco at night and every pub plays its own kind of music. And at full volume. The *Hotel Lovćen (180 rooms | tel. 030 37 44 44 | Moderate)* is a pleasant place to stay. The mediaeval church dedicated to Saint Tekla is an interesting cultural monument in Sutomore. An Orthodox and Catholic altar stand side by side as a sign of religious tolerance.

LOW BUDGET

▶ *Ekspres restorani* (self-service restaurants) were already popular in the Tito era and are an inexpensive option for a meal. Today there is one of these quick service restaurants, where you can fill up for comparatively little money, in most of the tourist centres. The one in Budva is in the venerable *Hotel Mogren (49 rooms | Slovenska obala 2 | tel. 033 45 11 02 | www.mogrenhotel.com)* at the entrance to the old town.

▶ The *Mesara* butcher shop *(Jadranski put | in front of the filling station | Budva)* will even grill the pieces of fillet beef you have just bought free of charge. A kilo of the meat is only 22 euros!

The town is crowded in the summer months – especially on weekends when all of Podgorica migrates to the coast.

ULCINJ (ULQIN)

(127 D6) (*ℳ R8*) **Nowhere else on the eastern Adriatic are the beaches as long and sandy as they are around Ulcinj (pop. 12,000), the southernmost town on the Montenegrin coast.**

From time immemorial, the sea has washed sand ashore that is rich in salts; created by the erosion of quartz boulders, it reaches the coast with the flow of the Montenegrin Albanian border river, the Bojana.

In addition to its beaches Ulcinj also draws tourists with its Oriental character. Starting in the Middle Ages, migrants from the Slavic principality of Zeta settled here along with Albanians coming from the south who now make up more than three quarters of the population.

SIGHTSEEING

GRADSKI MUZEJ (CITY MUSEUM)

The museum, housed in the old Turkish prison, shows many testimonies to the history of the city including old Muslim gravestones and Turkish cannonballs. *Mon–Sat 8am–2pm | at the western gate to the old town | entrance fee 1 euro*

STARI GRAD (OLD TOWN) ☆

The foundations of the old town, standing proudly above the newer part of Ulcinj, have their roots in Illyrian and Greek eras and were later altered time and time again by Byzantine, Turkish and Venetian inhabitants and conquerors. The cyclopean walls of the old citadel recall the splen-

Narrow alleys wind their way through Ulcinj's old town

dour of the ancient seafaring city that was captured by the Romans in the 2nd century BC and named Ocinium. The *Balšić Tower (Balšića kula)* on the other hand was built in the days of the mediaeval state of Raška.

FOOD & DRINK

Many Albanians have become successful restaurateurs and it is possible to choose between traditional Balkan cuisine *(ćevapčići* and *ražnjići)* and an excellent variety of fish in Ulcinj. No matter whether you select the *Aragosta (mobile 069 33 25 28 | Moderate)* with a view of the harbour or *Antigona (mobile 069 53 35 91 | Moderate)* in the old part of town or *Teuta* with its 1400ft² large terrace *(tel. 030 42 14 22 | Moderate)*, you will be delighted by their excellent value for money. You can also eat well and inexpensively in the numerous bars and pizzerias at the Grand Beach, *Velika plaža*.

LEISURE & SPORT

Ulcinj is an ideal location for surfers and divers. The winds here are stronger than in the north off Budva or Tivat and the hotels and camping sites to the south of the city are right behind the coast meaning that there is only the 50m/165ft wide stretch of sandy beach *Velika plaža* separating you from the waves.

BEACHES

CITY BEACHES

Gradska plaža, the city beach is also known as *Mala plaža* (the little beach) and is usually very crowded. There is deep water and several small beaches near the cliffs to the left of the sandy beach. A small nudist beach lies tucked away in the shade of some cypresses and there is also a very popular ladies' beach *Ženska plaža*

where the sulphur, radium and sea salts are said to have healing properties.

VELIKA PLAŽA (GRAND BEACH) ★ ●

Copacabana and Tropicana are two major sections of the longest beach in Montenegro that stretches for more than 12km/7.5mi to the Albanian border. They are ideal for small children who can splash around in the shallow water. The strong afternoon winds also make the beach ideal for experienced surfers.

WHERE TO STAY

Ulcinj promotes its large camping sites but they are rarely up to standard. Sometimes it is cheaper to opt for private accommodation; it is possible to pay less than 10 euros per night for a bed during the high season.

DVORI BALŠIĆA

Located in the heart of the old town of Ulcinj, the best hotel in town comprises the main stone building as well as two-storey apartments beneath the Balšić Tower. *19 rooms | tel. 030 42 14 57 | Moderate–Expensive*

LION

The Hotel Lion in *Štoj* – far away from the narrow streets of the old town of Ulcinj and surrounded by sand, the wind and

AGAINST THE CURRENT

When the large amount of water from the thaw of snow in the Albanian mountain regions makes the Bojana River's main tributary the Drim swell at the end of winter, the main river is no longer able to keep flowing in its customary direction.

Instead of flowing from Lake Skadar into the Adriatic, the river on the border of Montenegro and Albania starts to flow upstream. The fishermen who spread their trapeze nets in the Bojana Delta are then guaranteed fine catches!

the waves in the middle of the Grand Beach – has tasteful décor and attractive prices. *25 rooms | tel. 030 45 71 56 | www. hotellion-ul.com | Budget*

VILA TAMARA

The owner Tamara personally takes care of her guests' wishes. The small house is located above the city beach and has a

WHERE TO GO

ADA BOJANA (127 F6) *(M S8)*

The island in the delta of the Albanian Montenegrin border river 16km/10mi east of Ulcinj can only be reached from the mainland via a bridge. The **INSIDER TIP** longest nudist beach in Montenegro is here. It is part of the *Ada Bojana* hotel complex

On the island of Ada Bojana the fishermen still use these traditional suspended nets

unique view over Old Ulcinj and the spectacular sunsets. The two apartments (which accommodate up to six) are in a small garden full of agave and oleander. *Ivana Milutinovića | mobile 069 46 57 47 (June–Oct), tel. in Belgrade +381 11 2 77 47 70 (Nov–May) | Budget*

INFORMATION

TURISTIČKA ORGANIZACIJA ULCINJ

Bulevar Maršala Tita | tel. 030 41 23 33 | www.ulcinj.travel

(250 rooms | tel. 030 411 3 51 | Budget) and is reserved for guests staying there. The hotel has simple, reasonably priced rooms – most of them have now been renovated. There are also camping sites on Ada Bojana. Nothing is perfect on the island but – in spite of the middling accommodation – it has developed into a paradise for tourists who are nature and sports enthusiasts. The wind, water and sun also create ideal conditions for kite surfers. Further information is available at *www.kiteloop.net*

CETINJE, PODGORICA & LAKE SKADAR

The journey from Kotor to Cetinje offers one of the most beautiful views in Europe. You gain 1000m/3280ft in altitude in next to no time but negotiate about 30 hairpin bends enroute.

The incredible vista of the Bay of Kotor, surrounded by the karst formations of the Lovćen Mountains, opens up in for all to see. There are also old roads from the north, from Nikšić, Danilovgrad or the Bosnian border and Grahovo leading to Cetinje. The more than a century old network of roads show how important the city once was – and still is – for the residents in the region. It was the first capital of the new state established at the end of the 19th century after the freedom-loving Montenegrins had struggled against the Ottomans for centuries. Today, lively Podgorica is Montenegro's capital and its political, business and cultural centre.

Similar to the route over the Lovćen Mountains, the car ride on the old roads from Cetinje to Podgorica is another unforgettable highlight of any trip to Montenegro. Lake Skadar, down below on the plain, glitters in the sunlight in shades of green and dark blue. Hundreds of birds nest around the largest lake on the Balkan Peninsula. It is also an inexhaustible source of food for the people living around it, who were almost completely cut off from

Magnificent embassy buildings and quaint fishing villages: from the old capital to the shores of the largest lake in the Balkans

the cities on the coast until a few decades ago, and lived from fishing.

CETINJE

MAP INSIDE BACK COVER
(124 C3–4) (*L–M4*) ★ The historical capital city (pop. 15,000) feels like a large open air museum.

A city full of traces of the years after the first independence of Montenegro following the 1878 Congress of Berlin: embassies of all of the major powers of the time, who maintained contacts to King Nikola I, are scattered throughout the town. The king craftily saw that his daughters married into the courts of many of the continent's royal families and, in this way, made the small country more

A past reminder of Cetinje's political importance: the former Russian Embassy

influential than it would ever be again. The history of the community, built on a barren field of karst, dates back to the 15th century when the first Montenegrin ruler, Ivan Crnojević, established his residence here while retreating from the Turks. The spiritual and political leader had the monastery in Cetinje built in 1484. At the end of the 19th century the sleepy artists' metropolis was given the new appearance that it has retained to this day: low houses and straight streets lined with lime trees and acacias.

SIGHTSEEING

The city's central museum administration has its offices in the Government House (*Vladin dom*). This is where tourists can buy discount combi-tickets (5 euros) for the Montenegrin Art Gallery, the King Nikola Museum and the History Museum. The opening times of all the museums are: *mid April–Oct daily 9am–5pm, Nov–mid April Mon–Fri 9am–5pm | entrance fee 3 euros.*

BILJARDA (NJEGOŠ MUSEUM)

The former residence of the poet Prince Bishop Petar Njegoš includes books from the library of the spiritual and political leader, his own writings – including the manuscript of the 'The Mountain Wreath' – as well as the billiard table that was to give the building its name. It was transported on donkeyback up the stony road from Kotor at the beginning of the 19th century. *Trg Novice Cerovića*

EMBASSY BUILDINGS

Montenegro's recognition as an independent state in 1878 led to a great increase in Cetinje's international importance. The embassies of what were then the most powerful European states France (*Njegoševa*), Russia (*Vuka Mićunovića*), England (*Trg Novice Cerovića*) and the Austrio-Hungarian Empire (*Pivljanina*) are particularly impressive.

CRKVA NA ĆIPURU (CASTLE CHAPEL)

Erected on the ruins of the historical monastery that was destroyed in 1886, the small chapel now houses the coffins with the mortal remains of King Nikola I and Queen Milena.

ETNOGRAFSKI MUZEJ (ETHNOGRAPHIC MUSEUM)

The museum is located in the former Serbian embassy building. It exhibits Montenegro social history through the centuries with displays of weapons, traditional costumes and agricultural tools. *Trg Novice Cerovića*

MANASTIR (MONASTERY)

Reconstruction of this monastery, which was erected by the founder of the Montenegrin state, Ivan Crnojević, and destroyed by the Turks in 1692, began at the end of the 17th century. However, the Ottoman armies once again laid waste to Montenegro's religious centre in 1712 and 1785 before it could be restored in a more modest style in the years that followed. The monastery's treasury and shrine with relics of Saint Peter of Cetinje are especially worth seeing.

MUZEJ KRALJA NIKOLE (KING NIKOLA MUSEUM)

The former castle has been a museum since 1926: the ruler's parade, hunting and trophy weapons are displayed on the ground floor. A tour of the first floor, with the living quarters and work rooms decorated with the original furniture and paintings, gives an impression of the everyday life of the king. *Trg Novice Cerovića*

PLAVI DVORAC (BLUE CASTLE)

Prince Danilo's former residence in dazzlingly blue has a magnificent location in the city park. The building, which was constructed at the end of the 19th century, later served as the model for the other castles of the Montenegrin royal family.

UMJETNIČKA GALERIJA (ART MUSEUM)

The exhibition on the first floor of the Government House shows works by classical and modern Yugoslavian and Montenegrin artists. The collection dates back to the 17th century and also has works from past Biennales. The highlight of the exhibition is the *Icon of Mary the Mother of God by Philernmos*, the patron saint of the Order of Knights of St John, that is displayed in the Blue Chapel. The golden portrait is one of the most important sacred relics of Christianity. It is said that it was painted by Luke the Evangelist. *Vladin dom*

VLAŠKA CRKVA (VLAH CHURCH)

The oldest building in Cetinje (1450) is named after the shepherds who grazed their animals in the region. According to

MARCO POLO HIGHLIGHTS

★ **Cetinje**
The old capital city with the historic embassies is like an enormous open air museum
→ **p. 65**

★ **Lovćen Nacionalni Park**
The view from the country's major attraction stretches across the Adriatic as far as Italy → **p. 68**

★ **Njeguši**
The air-dried ham from this village is famous worldwide
→ **p. 68**

★ **Skadarsko jezero (Lake Skadar)**
Countless species of birds and an abundance of fish – a treasure trove of nature's riches → **p. 72**

legend the bones of the bandit chief Bajo Pivljanin and his wife, who lost their lives defending Cetinje against the Turks, are buried beneath the two tombstones in front of the church.

ZETSKI DOM (ROYAL THEATRE)
The building in the heart of Cetinje initially housed newly created cultural institutions that shot up like mushrooms in Montenegro in the wake of the Congress of Berlin: museum, library and theatre.

FOOF & DRINK

BELVEDER ☙
This restaurant that first opened its doors as a coffee house in 1888, from the terrace it boasts panoramic views that sweep across Lake Skadar as far as Albania. You should try the tasty lamb cooked under the *sač*. *On the main road, left before entering the city on the road from Podgorica | tel. 041 23 52 82 | Moderate*

WHERE TO STAY

GRAND
The original hotel building was destroyed in the 1979 earthquake. The new building on the site could never match the splendour of days gone by but the wooden-panelled rooms, sauna and swimming pool still guarantee a pleasant stay. *202 rooms | Njegoševa | tel. 041 23 16 51 | www.hotelgrand.me | Moderate–Expensive*

INFORMATION

TURISTIČKA ORGANIZACIJA CETINJE
Bajova 2 | tel. 041 23 92 50

WHERE TO GO

LOVĆEN NACIONALNI PARK ★ ☙
(124 A–C 3–4) (*ØØ L4–5*)
On a clear day, the view from the peaks in the national park stretches across the Mediterranean all the way to Italy. Njegoš, the poet prince, lies buried in an oversized mausoleum *(see p. 92)* on the second highest summit in the massif, the *Jezerski vrh* (1660m/5446ft). Adults and children can climb, slide, crawl and overcome obstacles in the 5 acres of the *Adventure Park (Avanturistički park Lovćen | mobile 069 54 31 56)* in Ivanova Korita

NJEGUŠI ★
(124 A4) (*ØØ L4*)
The birthplace (pop. 200) of the poet and Prince, Petar Njegoš, is 23km/14mi away from Cetinje towards the Bay of Kotor. A special smoking technique has made the ham produced by the farmers in the village famous far beyond the boundaries

WORLD-CLASS ART IN CETINJE

The world famous performance artist Marina Abramović, who has Montenegrin roots, is hoping to draw the international art scene to Cetinje by lending her name to the multifunctional centre for modern art – the *Marina Abramović Community Center Obod Cetinje (www. maccocetinje.me)*. An old refrigerator factory in Obod has been transformed by the Dutch architect Rem Koolhaas for the project. The plan is to use the centre to host opera and theatre performances and to also provide space for film studios and other artistic activities.

of Montenegro. You can also buy smoked cheese, wine and home-distilled spirits here – look for the signs *(pršut, sir, vino, rakija)*. The house Njegoš was born in is only open in summer and can be found – there is a signpost – on the main road. ☼ *Kod Pera Na Bukovicu (tel. 041

you between the two highest peaks in the Lovćen and back to Njeguši in approximately three and a half hours.

OBOD (125 D4) *( N5)*

The hamlet of Obod (pop. 200) lies on a small hill opposite Rijeka Crnojevića,

You should not miss out on this speciality: the famed Njeguši ham

76 00 55 | Budget), the oldest pub in the region, serves all of the local specialities – and also guarantees a spectacular view of the Lovćen.

Njeguši is the best place to set out on a hike on the Jezerski vrh, the second highest peak in the Lovćen Mountains and also the site of the Prince Njegoš' mausoleum. The path begins at a sharp curve to the left about 200m/656ft before Kod Pera Na Bukovicu. You can fill up on drinking water at the well and then set off on the old Austro-Hungarian horse trail towards the *Šanik* and *Trešnja* mountain huts. After Trešnja, the path goes to the southwest in the direction of Jezerski vrh until you reach a lake beneath the Lovćen. The path that takes you up to the summit is under a rocky cliff. The ascent lasts around four hours and the return hike will take

18km/11mi from Cetinje. Although there is still an Orthodox church and a few old stone houses, you will hardly see any people. In 1475, Prince Ivan Crnojević and his entourage escaped from the Turks by retreating from Lake Skadar to Obod. Only a few years after Johannes Gutenberg had invented book printing, Crnojević's son Đurađ established the first printing press in south-east Europe here in 1493; it was later transferred to Cetinje. The first book to be printed in Cyrillic letters was produced in Obod and, starting in 1494, there was a steady flow of *Oktoih,* the Book of Psalms, and a prayer book from the presses. However, the regime of the Crnojević dynasty ended a mere two years later: the Turkish conquest of the country was considered complete after Đurađ fled to Venice.

The old bridge over the Rijeka Crnojevića in the village of the same name

RIJEKA CRNOJEVIĆA (125 D3) (*ℳ N4*)
Those who take the old road from Cetinje to Podgorica will be rewarded with spectacular views of Lake Skadar. The river – which is also named *Rijeka Crnojevića* – with its beautiful green water winds its way into the lake. The tiny village itself, 16km/10mi east of Cetinje, does not have much to offer except an old Turkish bridge, *Stari most*, but you can eat well in the restaurant named after it *(mobile 069 33 94 29 | Expensive)*.

PODGORICA

MAP INSIDE BACK COVER
(120 C5) (*ℳ O2*) **In the early evening at the very latest, it will become clear where the heartbeat of the capital city (pop. 140,000) can be felt: all cars are banned from the zone between Freedom Street (Slobode) and Marka Miljanova after 5pm.**

After that, the area near the Parliament and National Theatre belongs to those out for a stroll. And anybody who stays longer here, and is not only passing through, soon learns to take a second look at things. All of a sudden, dozens of children come together to play basketball and football behind the endless blocks of housing on *Bulevar Svetog Petra Cetinjskog* and Podgorica becomes the capital city of spacious parks. Two rivers, the Morača and Ribnica, also flow through the middle of the metropolis and four others have their courses not far away – this is the reason that the first time it was mentioned it was called Ribnica (*ribe* = fish) before the city was renamed Podgorica (at the foot of the hill) in 1326. During Yugoslavia's Socialist period, the city in the fertile Zeta Valley was given the name of Titograd in honour of the special commitment of Montenegrin partisans before finally reverting to its old name in 1992.

SIGHTSEEING

CENTAR SAVREMENE UMJETNOSTI CRNE GORE ●
The works of Montenegrin modern artists are exhibited in the light-flooded rooms of the Centre for Contemporary Art on the city's central boulevard. The largest section of the collection is on display in the old winter palace of King Nikola in the city

CITY **WHERE TO START?**
Hotel Crna Gora: The historically interesting hotel on Bulevar Svetog Petra Cetinjskog is in the lively heart of the city. Around the corner, Slobode Street glitters with its elegant boutiques and there are any number of bars and bistros on Njegoševa Street. A few minutes away, visitors will be taken back to the past in Podgorica's old town. The train station is only ten minutes away by car and the drive from the airport to Crna Gora will only take around 15 minutes. It is easy to find parking on the street.

park where the Gallery of the Nonaligned States was housed until 1985. And even today, paintings from Montenegro and the other republics of former Yugoslavia still hang on the walls alongside works by artists from Bolivia, Egypt and Cuba. *Bulevar Svetog Petra Cetinjskog 17 (city centre) and Ljubljanska (winter palace) | Mon–Fri 9am–2pm and 5pm–9pm, Sat 10am–2pm | free admission*

GORICA ⋇

There is a fantastic view of the Morača and the stadium of the FK Budućnost (which means 'future') Podgorica football club from the northern hill and you will also be able to take a look inside the 12th century church *Sveti Đorđe* (Saint George).

STARA VAROŠ

The Ribnica River forms the boundary between the new *(nova)* and old *(stara)* sections of town. The days of Ottoman rule come back to life when one hears the Muezzin calling the faithful to prayer in the Stara Varoš quarter. The clock tower from the 17th century, *Sahat kula*, is one

of the few well-preserved examples of Islamic architecture in Podgorica. It is on *Trg Bećir Bega Osmanagića Square*. If you are wondering about the blue trimmed sheets of paper hanging here (and there on public buildings and other places in the town) they are ● death notices. In this way the people in Montenegro publicly mourn their loved ones.

FOOD & DRINK

INSIDER**TIP** KUŽINA

The 'kitchen' in the immediate vicinity of the Sahat kula serves traditional Montenegrin dishes from what people here call the 'lost times'. The specialities of the house include kid and lamb from the grill, local polenta and all kinds of sweet dishes. *Trg Božane Vučinić 2 | tel. 020 63 38 33 | Budget*

MAREZA

This restaurant on the northern outskirts of Podgorica has its own trout farm and serves its guests excellent local cuisine. *Mareza | tel. 020 28 10 09 | Moderate*

INSIDER**TIP** MAŠA

The elegant restaurant not only has homemade pasta but also local specialities prepared with great finesse on its menu. Try the delicious turkey in gorgonzola sauce! *Bulevar Svetog Petra Cetinjskog 31 | tel. 020 22 44 60 | Expensive*

ENTERTAINMENT

When the heat of day has finally become less stifling, the capital springs back to life in the magical square between *Stanka Dragojevića, Karađorđeva, Slobode* and *Hercegovačka*. This is where you will find the most bars and pubs; they cater to all tastes from the rustic beer hall *Pivnica*

(Stanka Dragojevića 12), to the hip *Buda Bar (Stanka Dragojevića 26)* and the trendy *Café Intercity (Njegoševa 40)* that is also open during the day.

KINO KULTURA ●

Foreign films are usually shown in English with Serbian subtitles. *Proleterske Brigade 1*

WHERE TO STAY

Hilton purchased the venerable Hotel *Crna Gora (Bulevar Svetog Petra Cetinj-skog 2)* in 2011, construction is underway and the new hotel is set to reopen in May 2015 as Hilton Montenegro. There is a wide selection of business hotels as many international companies and foreign embassies have offices in Podgorica. There are also numerous reasonably-priced apartments – most of them in the city centre. For example, the operators of a bed and breakfast hotel, the *Piramida (10 rooms | Ul. Nikole Tesle 26 | tel. 020 61 16 08 | Moderate)*, a little way out of town, also offer well-equipped apartments in the centre *(Budget–Moderate)*.

INSIDER TIP KERBER

This hotel is wonderfully tucked away in the heart of the city but still only a two minute walk from the hustle and bustle on the chic shopping street, the Sloboda. There is even a mini sauna available for an additional fee. *20 rooms | Novaka Miloševa 6 | tel. 020 40 54 05 | www.hotel kerber.me | Moderate*

LOVĆEN

Guests, dogs and cats are all welcome in this hotel 2km/1mi outside of Podgorica on the road from the airport. The prices are reasonable; there is internet access, TV and a large car park. *22 rooms | tel. 020 66 92 01 | www.hotellovcen.co.me | Moderate*

INFORMATION

NACIONALNA TURISTIČKA ORGANIZACIJA CRNE GORE
Bulevar Svetog Petra Cetinjskog 130 | tel. 077 10 00 01 | 24 hour information telephone 13 00 | www.montenegro.travel

WHERE TO GO

DUKLIJA (120 C5) *(ᴍ O2)*

The first Illyrian city conquered by the Romans is only 3km/2mi north of Podgorica, near the village of Rogami, the ruins include traces of an ancient sewage system along with the stone remains of baths and a basilica.

SKADARSKO JEZERO (LAKE SKADAR)

(126–127 A–F 1–3) *(ᴍ N–S 3–6)*

⭐ **Gardens covered in vines, dilapidated churches in the valley and white-walled cemeteries set in lush meadows and fertile fields: the residents of Lake Skadar live in harmony with nature and reap the benefits of its bounty.**

This body of water, which is named after the most important city on its shores Skadar (Albanian: Shkoder), is fed by subterranean springs and has the same temperature throughout the year. The lake is the largest on the Balkan Peninsula. After the snow thaw in spring, it expands to cover an area of more than 190 square miles and is still over 100 square miles in autumn. Its wealth of fish and great variety of birdlife are unequalled in Europe and make it a paradise for fans of flora and fauna. Pelicans, cormorants and herons have their breeding grounds

There are huge shoals of fish swim in Lake Skadar and lots of happy fishermen

here, thousand of migratory birds flock to the lake to escape the winter temperatures in the north and stay from late autumn until spring. The waters are also home to massive schools of carp, sardine-size bleak, salmon trout, pike and perch. In 1983 Montenegro realised that this habitat was worth protecting and part of the lake was declared a national park. The Albanian section has also been protected since 2005.

The lake is fed by the ice-cold water of the *Morača*, which flows into the Skadar on the west side. Rebellious Montenegrin clans and Turkish conquerors fought over the region for centuries. Today, the border between Montenegro and Albania runs down the middle of the lake.

It is really worth going out of your way to visit this unique habitat, which will give you some breathtaking pictures for your holiday album. The surface of the water is covered with rare plants and glitters in many colours. There is a wonderful fra-

grance from the laurel trees in **INSIDER TIP** *Mala Gorica* and the chestnut trees in *Limljani* soar up to the skies. The *Rijeka Crnojevića* river its winds its way fjord-like to the lake. Old fishing villages and convents where nuns dressed in black carry out their work in silence are the kinds of scenes from a world that is no more than two hours away from all of the hustle and bustle of the tourist towns on the coast.

WHERE TO GO ON LAKE SKADAR

BEŠKA ● **(126 C2–3)** *(ᗰ P–Q6)*
Swallows, snakes and stones – that was what constituted the tiny island in the southern part of Lake Skadar until 2004. Then Orthodox nuns arrived and settled in the convent that had been deserted for 300 years. They have had electricity for a few years now but there is still no running water. The barren island smells of rosemary and sage, the sun burns down and

the nuns work and pray until late at night. And, they welcome day-trippers who bring some change to their monotonous life. Two and eight hour boat trips are offered locally. Most of the excursion boats depart

The monument in Virpazar commemorates Montenegrin partisans

from Virpazar or Murići in the morning. Information is available from the Visitor Centre in Virpazar *(tel. 020 87 91 00)*.

LIMLJANI
(126 A3) *(∅ 06)*

Mr Sjekloća serves his guests the best his cellar has to offer in the small winery **INSIDER TIP** *Sjekloća Vino (visits by appointment only; mobile 069 02 02 85 | www.sjeklocavino.com)* in the village of Limljani. The wines have received many awards and the grappa is really potent but the prices are reasonable. A visit to

the estate and cellar, including wine tasting and a small snack, costs 50 euros.

A winding road through the mountains leads from Limljani to *Murići*, on the one side is the glittering lake and on the other a lunar landscape. Catholic churches and mosques stand side by side in the villages you pass through. After you leave Murići, the route takes you via *Mount Rumija* (1584m/5197ft) to Ulcinj and Ada Bojana.

PLAVNICA
(126 A–B1) *(∅ P4)*

An ultra-modern hotel complex *(Plavnica Eco Resort | 4 apartments | tel. 020 44 37 00 | www.plavnica.info | Expensive)* has been built in the village of Plavnica on the Podgorica side of Lake Skadar. The luxurious apartments are named after the last Montenegrin princesses. From the futuristic terrace, hotel guests have a view across the large swimming pool to the lake. Concerts, fashion events and beauty contests are also held here.

VIRPAZAR
(125 E–F5) *(∅ O5)*

Tourists will immediately see that the largest town (pop. 1000) on the Montenegrin shore of Lake Skadar held a strategically important position for centuries. It was once an island – and was the last bastion against the Turks. If you follow the dead-straight railway embankment that was built in the 1970s for a mile or so towards Podgorica, you will see the *Lesendra* fortress on the left-hand side. The Turkish stronghold was built to secure the conquests of the pashas in Istanbul. Today, two bridges connect the fishing village with the coast. The monument to the partisans hewn into the rock behind the bridge over the Crmnica commemorates another historical event. This is where the Montenegrin Communists, led by Josip

Broz Tito's comrade in arms Milovan Đilas, began their uprising against the Italian fascists on 13 July 1941. The weekly market that gave the village its name (Virazpar means 'lively market') is held on Friday and is full of colour. In a babble of Montenegrin and Albanian, peasant women and fishermen offer all of the natural delicacies the area has to offer from fresh olive oil to carp to tomatoes and peppers. The excursion boat season, for trips along the lake reeds, begins at the end of April when the irises and water lilies are in full bloom. At the entrance to the town is the down-to-earth restaurant, the INSIDER TIP *Pelikan (tel. 020 711107 | www.pelikan-zec.com | Budget–Moderate)*, the oldest in Virpazar. Ask to have a look at the kitchen with its traditional equipment on the top floor – metal tableware from the end of the 19th century and the open hearth over which the catch from the lake is smoked. There is also a fine selection of seafood from the Adriatic and eight inexpensive rooms *(Budget)* if you decide to spend the night.

INSIDER TIP ŽABLJAK

(126 A1) *(🕮 O4)*

It is possible that the myth of Montenegro's Black Mountain has its origins in this sleepy little village between rivers and the lake 23km/14mi from Virpazar. Before the Ottomans started making life difficult for the founder of the state Ivan Crnojević and his companions, they had their ancestral seat in this fortress on the edge of Lake Skadar – it was a safe haven in the midst of the hostility of nature. However, after the Turkish troops had conquered Podgorica and Skadar, the members of the Crnojević clan saw themselves forced to give up their vulnerable retreat on the plain and move to highlands of Obod and Cetinje at the end of the 15th century. A small trail leads up to the well-preserved ruins in 15 minutes. From the top there is a magnificent view of the enormous lake and river landscape – especially after the snow thaw in spring when the flowers are in full bloom. A memorial stone on the north-west wall commemorates the battle of 1835.

LEISURE & SPORT

Hikers and cyclists follow the 3.5km/2mi long *art tour*: a series of works by Montenegrin sculptors on the millers' path between the two villages of Poseljani and Smokovci. You can extend the tour as far as Rijeka Crnojevića. There is also a *wine route* between Virpazar and Rijeka. Anglers and bird lovers can explore the lake by boat. The visitor centres in Vranjina, Murići, Rijeka Crnojevića and Virpazar provide local information. The centre in Virpazar *(tel. 020 879100)* also rents hiking equipment.

LOW BUDGET

▶ In Montenegro, the summer sales last from June to August. Department stores such as *Robna kuća NIKIć (Kralja Milana 19)* in Podgorica offer brand-name articles at greatly reduced prices during this time.

▶ The village of Medun north-east of Podgorica is considered the 'capital' of the Kuči clan, which produced many freedom fighters. Marko Miljanov, the poet and a great 19th century hero, documented history of the clan and the ● *museum (daily 9am–7pm| free admission)* in his former residence provides information on his life and the Kučis.

THE NORTH-WEST

More than 20 mountain peaks over 2000m/6560ft high, more than a dozen glacial lakes and countless springs, brooks and rivers. To experience all of the pristine beauty the Montenegrin mountain region has to offer you should definitely plan to visit the area between Žabljak and Nikšić.

The Durmitor National Park offers mountain hikers a wide selection of routes – and, in winter, the ski slopes provide some of the best downhill runs on the Balkan Peninsula. A rafting trip on the Tara, the wild river of the north, has become something of a must for all visitors to Montenegro. A feast for the eyes at any time of the year: the Black Lake (*Crno jezero*) near Žabljak and the Ledena pećina (Ice cave) with their stalactites and stalagmites.

NIKŠIĆ

(120 B4) (*∅ U13*) The second largest city in Montenegro (pop. 58,000) has always been overshadowed historically by Podgorica and Cetinje.

Although Nikšić was known as 'the city of steel and beer' during the Tito era, not much remained of the steel industry after the Yugoslavian Wars and hardly any-

The area with the deepest gorges and highest mountains: untamed Montenegro awaits in the Durmitor Mountains and Tara Canyon

body drank the famous *Nikšićko pivo* that had been brewed here since 1896. It was not until the state-run brewery was sold that things started to look up – at least, for the beer brewers. The national tipple took off and the unemployment rate decreased. The KAP aluminium factory was less lucky: it has been sold four times since 2002. The number of employees dwindled from 16,000 to a mere 2000 in the 2012. A Turkish entrepreneur recently bought the works and promised to help get the city back on its feet.

On the outskirts of town is the palace of King Nikola and the ruins of the castle complex, built by the Turkish conquerors in the 15th century, a reminder of a more glorious past. Today concerts and plays are performed here in summer.

Hewn in the rocks, the Ostrog Monastery is considered sacred by Orthodox, Catholics and Muslims alike

SIGHTSEEING

SVETI VASILIJE OSTROŠKI (ST VASILIJE CHURCH)

The house of worship, which was consecrated in 1900, is located next to the Royal Palace. It was erected in honour of the soldiers from the area who fell in the battle against the Turks in 1878.

UTVRĐENJE (FORTRESS)

The approximately 200m/656ft long, relatively well-preserved fortress at the western entrance to Nikšić was erected by the Ottoman rulers in the 16th century; it is now used in summer as a stage for musicians and actors.

ZAVIČAJNI MUZEJ GRADA NIKŠIĆA

The local heritage museum is housed in the former palace of King Nikola. The two floors of exhibits from the 18th and 19th centuries – and especially the reign of King Nikola – bring the past back to life. *Mon–Sat 10am–1pm | Trg Šaka Petrovića 1 | entrance fee 2 euros*

FOOD & DRINK

There are many small pubs and bistros in the centre of town. Apart from them, the few good restaurants are found in the hotels such as the *Trebjesa* and *Onogošt*. The meals are usually hearty, the servings large and the prices low. The regional specialities include apple and pear brandy.

WHERE TO STAY

ONOGOŠT

A genuine Socialist building in the centre. Everything is a bit rundown but still in working order. *189 rooms | Njegoševa 24 |*

tel. 040 24 28 60 | www.htponogost.me |
Moderate–Expensive

TREBJESA
This small hotel (newly renovated at great cost) lies a short way away from the city centre but this is compensated for by its idyllic location in a pine forest. *8 rooms | tel. 040 73 11 44 | www.hoteltrebjesa.me | Moderate–Expensive*

TURISTIČKA ORGANIZACIJA NIKŠIĆ
Slobode 9 | tel. 050 43 11 09

OSTROG ★ ●
(120 C4) *(* *U13)*
At first glance, the walls of the small room where the body of Saint Vasilije is preserved looks like they are covered in tattoos: frescoes of the saints have been painted directly on to the stone as one last sign of respect for the builder of the monastery. In 1665, the then Metropolitan of Herzegovina, Vasilije Ostrovski had the white building hewed into the rock after he had fled from the Turks and been forced to abandon his ancestral seat further to the west. Later the sanctuary, 22km/14mi away from Nikšić, became a place of pilgrimage for believers from all parts of former Yugoslavia. Many Orthodox families still have their children christened here – as was the case with the Bosnian-Serbian wartime President Radovan Karadžić who was born in Montenegro and who stood trial before the UN Tribunal in The Hague in 2012. Even Catholics and Muslims consider the place holy.
The motel **INSIDER TIP** *Koliba Bogetići (mobile 069 60 39 86 | www.kolibe.me | Moderate)* is only 8km/5mi from Ostrog

on the road towards Danilovgrad and Podgorica. The traditional food is excellent, the service friendly and the fresh air invigorating.

ŽABLJAK

(120 C2) *(* *V12)* **The highest town (at 1450m/4757ft) in Montenegro is also a centre of mountain tourism and winter sports – with many ideal excursion destinations in the immediate vicinity.**
Although Žabljak was destroyed several times during the Second World War, the typical mountain houses with their steep roofs still make this small community (pop. 2000) a charming place to visit. When the early morning mist rises from the Black Lake and disappears between

MARCO POLO HIGHLIGHTS

★ **Ostrog**
The white monastery in the rocks is an important sanctuary for Orthodox Christians
→ p. 79

★ **Durmitor Nacionalni Park**
Unspoiled nature at an altitude of more than 2000m/6560ft: Durmitor is the most beautiful national park in Montenegro
→ p. 81

★ **Piva**
The walls of this mediaeval monastery are decorated with countless frescoes → p. 82

★ **Tara**
Be carried away by the rapids on a rafting trip through the deepest canyon in Europe
→ p. 83

the peaks of the Bobotov kuk and the other mountains (over 2000m/6560ft high), it is hard to believe that people have ever put foot here.

FOOD & DRINK

DURMITOR
The bread is still baked in-house, the lambs and sheep come from the villages on the Durmitor – and so does the cheese. The restaurant is particularly suitable for large groups as there is plenty of room on the spacious terrace. *Vuka Karadžića 5 | mobile 069 63 73 16 | Moderate*

MB
The most elegant restaurant in town is part of the hotel with the same name and serves excellently prepared fish from the rivers and lakes in the region. *Tripka Đakovića | tel. 052 36 16 01 | Budget–Moderate*

SHOPPING

The makeshift market stalls that used to be set up on the pavements were recently banned from Žabljak. **INSIDER TIP**

LOW BUDGET

▶ Keep your eyes open for farmers selling sheep and goats cheese at the farmers' markets! It costs under 8 euros a kilo here.

▶ The word *pečenjara* means grill kiosk. Lamb chops, knuckle of pork or *ćevapčići* and *pljeskavica* are freshly prepared and inexpensive. It is easy to find them in many towns and villages – just follow the aroma of garlic and smoke.

Products from the mountain region, as well as shoes and clothing from all over the world, are now sold in the new, bright indoor daily market. On the ground floor farmers from the nearby villages sell cheese, potatoes and herbs, and even thick home-made pullovers (using wool from their own sheep). The first floor is reserved for boutiques, bookshops and bistros. The farmers leave the market hall in the early afternoon but the shops there remain open until 8pm.

LEISURE & SPORT

Sport and leisure activities play a major role in the development of Montenegro's north for tourism. There is a long list of possible activities: rafting, Jeep safaris, mountain biking, canyoning excursions and paragliding, as well as horseback rides, angling, and eco tours can all be booked through various tour operators. The majestic, unspoiled natural landscape of the north-west is unique and offers ideal conditions for all these activities. *Eco-Tours (Ul. Dunje Đokić | mobile 067 25 90 20 | www.eco-tours.co.me)* has their offices in Kolašin in the north-east but also has the best offers for this part of the country.

WHERE TO STAY

JEZERA
Located at the end of the ski lift, this establishment has a special Socialist charm, bright rooms and very helpful staff. There is a swimming pool, sauna and table tennis in the cellar. *149 rooms, 8 bungalows | Njegoševa | tel. 052 36 02 06 | www.hm-durmitor.com | Moderate*

MB
The well-maintained hotel has attractive rooms with warm pine panelling making

In the Durmitor Mountains the Bobotov kuk peak soars up more than 2500m/8200ft

it the best in town. *22 rooms | Tripka Đakovića | tel. 052 36 16 01 | www.mb hotel-mn.com | Budget–Moderate*

AUTOCAMP RAZVRŠJE

According to the owner of this camping site, Mišo Vojinović, anybody over the age of 80 who travels here with at least one parent can stay free of charge! However, the majority of the guests will be more interested in the special prices he offers for various groups. His mother bustles about in the kitchen where she ● bakes bread and cooks meals for the campers. Those who do not want to spend the night in their own tent can opt for one of the rustic huts. Vojinović also offers a variety of tours for his guests. *Mobile 067 44 44 77*

TURISTIČKA ORGANIZACIJA ŽABLJAK
Trg Durmitorskih ratnika 3 | tel. 052 36 18 02

WHERE TO GO

DURMITOR NACIONALNI PARK ★
(120–121 B–D 2–3) (*U–W 11–12*)

In 1980 Durmitor National Park was declared a Unesco World Heritage Site. Its area of 150 square miles offers all that any nature lover could desire: deep canyons, high mountains, caves, glacial lakes and a boundless variety of flora and fauna. The area around Žabljak alone has around 1300 species of plants and it is also a paradise for bird lovers. The park extends over a high plateau at an altitude of around 1500m/5000ft with even higher peaks rising up. Climbers have five huts at their disposal within the national park as well as accommodation options in *Škarka, Šušica*, at the *Sedlo* mountain saddle and some limited possibilities in *Lokvice* and *Velika Kalica*. You can spend the night in cosy peasant huts at the *Black Lake (Crno jezero)* in summer and winter and rent private rooms locally.

Over centuries the Tara has cut a deep canyon in the rocks

Ledena pećina (Ice Cave) at an altitude of more than 2000m/6560ft. There is a further steep path up to the ☽ *Velika Previja,* lookout point where you can also catch your breath at a spring. And then, it is only another 45 minutes to the peak of the Bobotov kuk. You make the downward hike from Velika Previja via *Zeleni Vir* and *Urdeni Do* to *Dobri Do* or the mountaineers' house in *Sedlo.*

PIVA ★ (120 B2) (𝄢 U12)

This monastery (55km/34mi from Žabljak) has a chequered history: in order to prevent the the 16th century three-nave church falling victim to the dam being constructed in Plužine, people began dismantling it bit by bit and rebuilding it at its current location in 1969. This action took just as long as the initial construction of the church. The walls are covered with frescoes; the paintings cover an area of more than 10,700ft². Pay particular attention to the INSIDER TIP▶ fresco over the south entrance: unique in Orthodox churches, it shows a picture of the Turkish Pasha Mehmed Sokolović, a relative of the Serbian patriarch at the time who had converted to Islam.

PLJEVLJA (120–121 C–D1) (𝄢 V11)

Foreign tourists rarely venture out on the journey to the most north-westerly city (pop. 19,000) in Montenegro around 60km/37mi from Žabljak. However, the trip is really worthwhile. Not only to admire the town's landmark – the Hussein Pasha Mosque *(Husein pašina džamija)*, with its tall slender minaret was erected shortly after the Turkish conquest in the 16th century – but also to explore the traces of ancient Illyrian and Roman settlements in the vicinity. Archaeologists found the remains of a Roman town near the hamlet of *Komine* but were only able to decipher the first letter of its name. The site is now

There is a demanding hike from Žabljak to the highest peak in the Durmitor Mountains, the *Bobotov kuk* (2523m/8278ft), that takes around seven hours. The path begins 3km/2mi outside of the village at Crno jezero, where a signpost indicates the marked route to *Indjini Dolovi*. After approximately four hours of hiking through karst craters and scree, you arrive at the

known as *Municipio S*. Finds from the Iron Age were uncovered in *Gotovuša*. And, not to be forgotten: the monks in the early 16th century Trinity Monastery *(Manastir Sveta Trojica)* in the centre of Pljevlja, who have one of the richest collections of icons, historical documents and books on the entire Balkan Peninsula. You will find simple rooms and the best cooking in the area at the *Hotel Gold (9 rooms | Miljanova | tel. 052 32 31 02 | Moderate)*.

TARA ★
(120–121 B–D 1–4) *(⊞ U–W 11–13)*

This is not only the longest river in the country, it is also one of the most beautiful: the Tara winds its way for 158km/98mi through the Montenegrin landscape, cutting through rocks and, shortly after Leveri, plunging 1300m/4265ft down a dozen cascades. The river has created the deepest canyon in Europe and – after the Grand Canyon – the second deepest worldwide; reason enough for the Unesco to declare the Tara a World Heritage Site in 1977. A few miles further on, it converges with the Piva and becomes the Bosnian-Serbian border river the Drina. Ivo Andrić, winner of the Nobel Prize for Literature, immor-

talized this in his city saga 'The Bridge on the Drina'. This wild river, which the Montenegrins have christened the 'Tear of Europe', flows so slowly near the town of *Bistrica* that one can even wade through the water. This place has been nicknamed the 'Devil's Lies' because the locals claim that it is possible to leap from one side to the other with a single jump.

The Montenegrins believe that everyone should down the Tara – in a kayak, boat or on an inflatable raft – at least once in a lifetime. The view from high up is also spectacular. In 1941, the bridge builder Lazar Janković spanned the ☞ Tara Bridge 150m/ 492ft high above the river shortly after *Đurđevića* (25km/16mi east of Žabljak). Just one year later, he blew up the central arch in an attempt to prevent the advance of the German National Socialist troops. Snack booths and a memorial invite visitors to make a stop for a rest.

The tour company **INSIDER TIP** *Explorer (Mojkovačka | mobile 067 26 31 38 | www. montenegroexplorer.co.me)* has its headquarters in Kolašin but offices can be found all over the north of Montenegro. The company's expert staff organises tours on the rivers and in the mountains.

CHURCH CONTROVERSY

There are churches, monasteries and chapels all over the north of Montenegro; many of them are decorated with magnificent frescoes and icons. Three quarters of the Montenegrins are Orthodox Christians – the exegesis of Christianity that was promoted by the Patriarch of Constantinople after the division of the Roman Empire and finally sealed with the Schism between Byzantium and Rome in1054. The Montenegrin

Orthodox Church lost its independence when the country became part of Yugoslavia in 1918. The church was more or less controlled by the state in the Tito era after 1945. In 1993, the Montenegrin Orthodox Church once again split with its Serbian Orthodox brothers in Belgrade who did not recognise this move. Since then, the two religious communities have been in dispute with no resolution in sight.

THE NORTH-EAST

Mountains over 2000m/6560ft high with their peaks capped with snow until well into summer, deep valleys, crystal-clear rivers and shimmering blue lakes: there is a new surprise around every corner in this area where four countries – Serbia, Albania, the Kosovo and Montenegro – come together.

Those in search of peace and quiet, away from the overcrowded tourist resorts on the Adriatic, will find it here in the fresh alpine air. And that at any time of the year – no matter whether it is on one of the numerous hiking trails through the Bjelasica Mountains, along the Mrtvica and Morača canyons or skiing downhill from Mount Ćupović. And there is even more to discover: hidden away in the north-eastern highlands between Kolašin, Bijelo Polje and Berane is the Biogradska gora National Park with one of the last primeval forests in Europe. And, in the centre is Biogradsko jezero, the enchanted glacial lake that gave the national park its name, where the mirrored reflection of the sky on the lake shimmers on its waters. More than anywhere else in Montenegro, the traces of Turkish rule have remained alive in the Sandžak region: you will hear the Muezzins calling the faithful to pray from the minarets of centuries-old mosques.

Photo: Biogradsko jezero

Ski slopes and environmental protection: a Mecca for winter sports enthusiasts and one of the oldest nature reserves in the world

BIJELO POLJE

(121 E3) (⊙ W12) **This city (pop. 17,000) is just 20km/12mi from the Serbian border. Its name means 'white field' after the splendid mass of wild flowers that adorn Bijelo Polje every year in spring.**

But the hilly landscape around the community on the banks of the River Lim is also completely white in winter: the skiing region in the Bjelasica Mountains is only a short distance away.

Founded in the 12th century, Bijelo Polje soon developed into a cultural and religious centre. It is on the banks of the third-longest river in Montenegro, the Lim that flows northwards towards Serbia. The city, which is surrounded by countless springs, became a bishop's seat in 1321

Kolašin is a good starting point for your expedition into the wild north-east of Montenegro

but came under Turkish control shortly thereafter.

members of the Christian faith were not able to worship in it again until 1912.

SIGTHTSEEING

SVETI NIKOLA (ST NICHOLAS CHURCH)
The church on the bank of the Lim River has a library from the 14th century where dozens of valuable manuscripts and early printed books are housed.

INSIDER TIP ▶ SVETI PETAR (ST PETER'S CHURCH)
One of the most important Orthodox manuscripts was created in this church at the end of the 12th century: the so-called Miroslav Gospel. A copy of the document is on display in the nave of the church while – much to the annoyance of the locals – the original is kept in the Serbian capital Belgrade. The whitewashed church tower was once used as a minaret: after the Turks conquered the city, they converted the church into a mosque and

FOOD & DRINK

There are restaurants and cafés in the centre of the small town. Most offer 'continental cuisine' with a lot of meat and not many vegetables. The prices are fairly reasonable wherever you eat.

WHERE TO STAY

DOMINUS
The well-appointed hotel is five minutes away from the centre of town. It provides free internet access. *Đorđija Stanića 31 | tel. 050 43 27 33 | Budget–Moderate*

INFORMATION

TURISTIČKA ORGANIZACIJA BIJELO POLJE
Slobode 9 | tel. 050 43 11 09

KOLAŠIN

(121 D4) *(ℳ W13)* **This is the most important winter sports town (pop. 6000) in the north-east of Montenegro and lies at an altitude of 960m/3150ft. It is also the country's water divide.**

While the Tara flows towards the Drina and then to the Black Sea by way of the Danube, the Morača's course is towards the Adriatic. During the Second World War, Tito's partisans founded their anti-fascist council here. Its proximity to the Bjelasica ski centre and Biogradska gora National Park makes Kolašin an ideal starting point to discover all the north-east has to offer.

The so called 'sheet cheese', made of layers of cream, is produced in the region around Kolašin. The *Putevi sira* ● INSIDER TIP *cheese tour* takes tourists to the farms where it is made. More information can be found under: *www.montenegro-mountains. com/cheese-routes*.

FOOD & DRINK

INSIDER TIP SAVARDAK
The name says it all: *Savardak* are the pyramid-like highlands huts and the restaurant (on the way out of town towards the Bjelasica ski centre) is housed in one of them. The restaurant specialises in hearty grilled food and the drinks are cooled outside in the brook. *Biocinovići | mobile 069 05 12 64 | Budget*

SPORTS & ACTIVITIES

BJELASICA SKI CENTRE
You will search in vain to find slopes this empty or prices this low anywhere in the Alps. The ski area 8km/5mi from Kolašin has one chairlift and three t-bars, a day pass costs 14 euros and you will only have to pay 104 euros for a weekly ticket. There are also two ski rentals where you will be charged 13 euros a day for boots, skies and poles. The hotels in the town organise transport to and from the centre.

WHERE TO STAY

BIANCA RESORT & SPA
A contemporary wood and stone construction with a gigantic swimming pool, spa and wellness complex set in the heart of the mountains. The elegant establishment is one of the best hotels in the country. *115 rooms | tel. 020 86 30 00 | www.bianca resort.com | Moderate–Expensive*

ČILE
The rustically decorated house also has a restaurant that serves traditional food. *9 rooms | Braće Milošević | tel. 020 86 50 39 | www.hotelcile.me | Budget– Moderate*

★ **Biogradska Gora Nacionalni Park**
Unwind in one of the world's oldest protected ecological areas surrounded by primeval forests and glacial lakes → p. 88

★ **Manastir Morača**
The magnificent frescoes in this important 13th century monastery bear witness to the influence of the Serbian Orthodox Church in the Middle Ages → p. 89

★ **Plav**
A delightful contrast: mosques from the 18th century and an alpine lake between mountains that tower over 2000m/6560ft → p. 89

MARCO POLO HIGHLIGHTS

VILA JELKA

The 'Fir Villa' is more than just a charming family pension. They also offer a winning combination: spend the night in wooden huts and then enjoy a wholefood meal including fish and meat from the region. The leisure activities include rafting, hiking and Jeep tours. *8 rooms | tel. 020 86 01 50 | www.vilajelka.co.me | Budget–Moderate*

INFORMATION

TURISTIČKA ORGANIZACIJA KOLAŠIN
Mirka Vešovića | tel. 020 86 42 54

WHERE TO GO

The small towns in the area around Kolašin, such as *Rožaje* (121 F4) (*∅ X13*) (pop. 10,000, 70km/43mi away) and *Andrijevica* (121 E4) (*∅ W13*) (pop. 1000, 45km/28mi to the east), have also developed into centres of tourism. You can ski here in winter and nature lovers and sports enthusiasts will also find plenty of activities to keep them busy in summer. The tourism office in Rožaje *(Maršala Tita | tel. 051 27 01 58)* and the website for the region *(www.bjelasica-komovi.co.me)* provide comprehensive information.

LOW BUDGET

▶ *Pita*, the typical, salty, Montenegrin turnovers filled with meat, cheese or spinach, are popular – and cheap – everywhere in the country. You will also find them in all the corner bakeries *(pekara)* in the north-east. The tasty snack costs between 1–2 euros; the locals usually have a glass of drinking yoghurt to go with it.

BERANE (121 E4) (*∅ X13*)
In Tito's Yugoslavia, Berane (43km/27mi to the east) was renamed Ivangrad after a heroic son of the city Ivan Milutinović fought as a partisan against the Germans in the Second World War. The sleepy backwater flourished under Tito: factories were built and the people had work. However, when Yugoslavia disintegrated, this prosperity disappeared along with the name. Today, Berane (pop. 35,000) is one of the poorest communities in Montenegro.

But that does not detract from the idyllic location; the small town (at an altitude of almost 700m/2300ft) on the banks of the River Lim is surrounded by mountains. The well-preserved 13th century monastery *Đurđevi stupovi* is not far away. You can spend the night at the reasonably priced, newly constructed *Il Sole Hotel (Polimska 17 | tel. 051 23 12 70 | www.ilsolehotel.com | Moderate)*. About 100m/300ft from the bank of the Lim is Il Sole restaurant *(Budget)* popular with the locals for its tasty and inexpensive food. Information: *Tourism Organisation Berane | Mojsija Zečevića 8 | tel. 051 23 66 64*

BIOGRADSKA GORA NACIONALNI PARK ★ (121 D–E 3–4) (*∅ W12–13*)
One of the last primeval forests in Europe is within the nature reserve (15km/9mi north-east) that was declared a national park in 1952. Preserving so much unspoilt nature in such a small area is not least thanks to Prince Nikola I. As early as in 1878, only six years after Yellowstone National Park was established in the America, he proclaimed Biogradska gora an environmentally protected area. The lakes here, which are known as 'eyes of the mountain' *(gorske oči)* are particularly interesting. The loveliest is *Lake Biogradsko (Biogradsko jezero)*. Eco-Tours *(Ul. Dunje Đokić | Kolašin | mobile 067 25 90 20 | www.eco-tours.co. me)* have a wide variety of activities on

offer including hikes in the park, or exploring it on a bicycle, on horseback or in a Jeep.

MANASTIR MORAČA ★
(121 D4) (*山 V13*)

Morača Monastery, built in 1252, is one of the most important Serbian Orthodox monasteries – both historically and artistically. It lies approximately 30km/19mi south-west of Kolašln, just after the confluence of the Mrtvica and Morača Rivers. The frescoes that were painted in the 16th and 17th centuries, after the church had been plundered by the Turks, make a visit particularly worthwhile. *Daily 8am–6pm | free admission*

PLAV ★ (121 E5) (*山 X14*)

The *Vezirova Mosque* from 1741 and the *Redžepagića Mosque,* which was built three decades later, are the main architectural highlights of Plav (pop. 2000, 63km/39mi to the south-east). The *Kula Redžepagića* defensive tower of the former ruling family is just up the hill from the mosque. The 2000m/6560ft long and 1400m/4600ft wide mountain lake *Plavsko jezero* is tucked away in the dense forests close to the town. It lies at the foot of Mount Prokletije (2700m/8858ft), which is known as the 'cursed mountain' because of its steep, bare walls.

Plav is an excellent starting point for cross-border hiking tours in Montenegro, Albania and the Kosovo. The transnational 'Peaks of the Balkans Trail' is a demanding hike from Plav into the Prokletije region, one of the most isolated mountain areas in the western Balkans. The trekking tour passes through spectacular landscapes, barren mountain massifs, secluded lakes, waterfalls, alpine pastures full of flowers and picturesque mountain villages. It reaches an altitude of 2300m/7546ft and forms a circular route of 192km/119mi and takes around ten days accompanied by experienced mountain guides. Mountaineering experience, surefootedness and first-class equipment are absolutely essential. Further information on the hike can be found at: *www.peaksofthebalkans. com*. Information: *Turistička organizacija Plav | Racina | tel. 051 25 28 88*

Magnificent frescoes in the Morača Monastery

TRIPS & TOURS

The tours are marked in green in the road atlas, the pull-out map and on the back cover

1 FROM THE COAST TO THE KARST

🚗 The Montenegrin landscape is spectacular wherever you go in the country but one part of the country has an incredible concentration of beauty – the Bay of Kotor. From the sea steep slopes soar upwards and the silhouettes of the little old Venetian villages are blurred on the clear water the higher up you drive. And, hardly has the Adriatic disappeared from sight, the landscape changes once again: karst mountains now dominate the scenery. This inaccessible area is where the Montenegrin

rulers withdrew to in the 15th century – in order to escape the Turkish conquerors – and establish their capital city, Cetinje. The day tour from Kotor to Budva, with a detour to visit the Njegoš Mausoleum, is around 120km/75mi long.

Leave **Kotor** → p. 40 at the southern exit out of town and, after around 4km/2.5mi, you reach a junction, go left and drive uphill towards Cetinje. This is also the start of the so-called ★ ⛟ **Ladder of Cattaro**, the road that provided the only access to the interior of the country until the end of the 19th century. It has long since been surfaced and now winds its way upwards offering a series of breathtaking

In tiny Montenegro all the highlights are close to each other, so leave the beach and set out to explore the interior!

views of the Bay of Kotor. Legend has it that the engineer who built the road was hopelessly in love with Queen Milena and hid an M in the 32 hairpin bends.

The most ☀ spectacular view over the expanse of the bay is just prior to **INSIDER TIP** the hamlet of **Krstac**. But there are a number of small lay-bys on the way up where you can stop to admire the scenery. It is now a good 2km/1mi from Krstac to

Njeguši → p. 68. In the birthplace of the poet Prince Njegoš you should taste the area's famous smoked ham and cheese produced by the local farmers. After leaving Njeguši, the road towards Cetinje continues upwards and passes fields below the two highest ☀ peaks in the Lovćen, the Štirovnik and Jezerski vrh. If the weather is clear, you will be able to see as far as the Goija Mountains in the north-west of Montenegro. You should reach **Cetinje → p. 65** in just under half an hour. A short stroll along the smart shopping street, Njegoševa, will give you a good idea of what life is like in the country's cultural capital of Cetinje.

You should now make a detour from Cetinje to the **Lovćen National Park → p. 68**. The almost 20km/13mi long route is well sign-

further to the west, through the karst highlands, towards the coast. Just when you think it cannot possibly go any higher, the Riviera appears in all its glory at the foot of the mountain. White bays and coves nestled between rocks, Budva, Petrovac na Moru with Sveti Stefan, the picturesque hotel island, in between. It is now only around 20minutes to the final

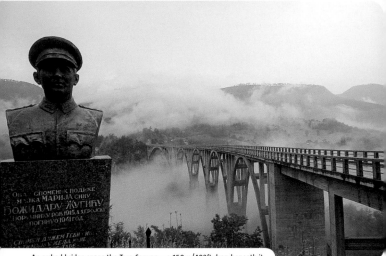

An arched bridge spans the Tara Canyon – a 150m/492ft drop beneath it

posted from the north-western end of town. After decades of construction, the oversized ● **Njegoš Mausoleum** *(8am– 6pm | entrance fee 2 euros)*, designed by the Croatian sculptor Ivan Meštrović, was opened on the second highest peak, the Jezerski vrh, in 1974. The chapel selected by poet himself as his burial place had more moderate dimensions. There is an ⛰ observation platform near the building and on a clear day there are panoramic views all the way to the mountains in Albania.

Driving down from Mount Lovćen, the route once again takes you over Cetinje

destination of the excursion, the fairytale old town of **Budva → p. 52**. But, of course, you can also continue on to **Tivat → p. 45** if you so wish. And the return trip back to your starting point in Kotor is only a thirty minute drive from Budva.

2 THE CANYONS ON THE TARA RIVER

Far away from the tourist resorts on the coast, the north of Montenegro offers some remarkable, unspoiled landscapes. The absolute highlight of this secluded mountain world: a trip down the stunning Tara River. The river becomes increasingly narrow after Kolašin and finally flows towards the Bosnian border in a series of raging rapids. The half-day excursion from Žabljak in the heart of the Durmitor Mountains passes Mojkovac to the Biogradska gora National Park where there are numerous trails for a hike in one of the last primeval forests in Europe. It is only around 90km/56mi from Žablak to the entrance to the park.

After you have left Bobotov kuk, the road from Žabljak → p. 79 towards Tara soon goes rapidly downhill. The stretch is lined with pine trees until you catch the first glimpse of the longest river in the country after 22km/14mi, at this point there are snack bars and a restaurant next to the 150m/492ft high arched bridge across the Tara.

Just before you arrive at Bistrica, the road curves away from the Tara and winds up the mountain – a ☀ panoramic lookout point has been set up here and you will have a spectacular panoramic view of the river flowing in its full width through the valley.

The road then once again follows the river all the way to Mojkovac before turning off to the south in the direction of Kolašin at the large partisan monument just before you reach the town. Today, Mojkovac is rather nondescript but it is a historical site where countless battles were fought. It used to be the only place where invaders, coming from Serbia or the Kosovo, could make inroads into Montenegro.

It is now only 2km/1mi until you reach the Biogradska gora National Park → p. 88. Signposts guide you to the car park at Lake Biogradsko with in a wooden kiosk where you can purchase a hiking guide. They also offer tours to the glacial lakes in the park, as well as accommodation

on the lakeside: the park administration provides twelve bungalows (*Budget*).

3 THE HEART AND SOUL OF MONTENEGRO

The name of this 140km/87mi long tour in Montenegrin is 'Putevima stare Crne Gore', loosely translated as 'old paths through natural Montenegro' which sounds a little less bombastic than the English title 'Old Royal Montenegrin Trails'. However, both indicate that, among other things, we are also dealing with the country's history. What they do not reveal is that this will also be a chance to get to know the locals. Far away from the main tourist routes between Lake Skadar, Podgorica, Nikšić and Cetinje, there are still people who cultivate their own farms and live from what they produce. These folk are the soul of Montenegro and their hospitality and warmth are legendary. You can reach them by car, bicycle or on a hike.

This project, which was initiated by the Ministry of Tourism (subsidised by the EU), has the aim of breathing new life into deserted farms, igniting the spirit of enterprise in small family businesses and developing environmentally-friendly tourism away from the main resorts. Farms were renovated, vineyards brought back into operation, and the number of bees needed to produce honey increased. The tour has been organised in a way that you can visit each individual farm with its historical highlight. It is possible to spend one or two days on the road or, if you want to, you can undertake the whole excursion in one piece. The routes are marked 'Etno-gastronomske staze'. The farmers provide special three-course meals for their guests at a price of only 10 to 15 euros per person. There are also packages offering food and drink and other activities; you can find out more details about these on site. It is also possible to spend the night on some of the farms; this also costs from 10 to 15 euros per person. Groups are welcome everywhere but they should reserve in advance. Detailed information is available from

a varied programme of activities including a tour of the wine cellars, a hike and a dip in the mountain river that flows right past the door. It is also possible to visit two monasteries. The complex in the village itself is especially worth seeing. The monastery in **Gornji Brčeli** dates back to the 15th century.

From Rijeka Crnojevića the eponymous river winds its way to Lake Skadar

the following website: *www.ethnogastro-balkan.net.*
The first stopover after you set out from **Virpazar → p. 74** is the village of **Donji Brčeli** on the old road to Petrovac na Moru. The Kopitović family *(mobile 067 21 20 44)* has lived here since the 15th century; their *konoba* (tavern) is three hundred years old. Visitors are treated to

Continue driving along the old road to Rijeka Crnojevića until you arrive at **Gornji Ceklin**, where Danilo Vukmirović's family *(mobile 069 06 07 59)* produces wine, honey and brandy. Depending on the season, you can help to harvest fruit or grapes or watch the bee-keeper extracting honey. It is also possible to spend the night on the family's farm. The areas around Donji Brčeli and Gornji Ceklin are ideal places to collect ● herbs. The mint, thyme and rocket that the hard-working farmers sell at the markets throughout Montenegro grow wild here.

Rijeka Crnojevića → p. 70 was once the seat of the ruler Ivan Crnojević. This is the starting point for hikes to the village of Smokovci or to the Obod Cave. Duško Jovićević's restaurant, *Mostina (mobile 069 84 33 17)*, is located right on the river and serves home-made brandy as well as fresh fish from the Rijeka. The secluded village of Obod → p. 69 is not far from Rijeka Crnojevića and is well worth a visit; this is where the first printing operation in south-east Europe was established in the 15th century.

The picturesque hamlet of Karuč has a lovely location on the shore of Lake Skadar on the old road to Cetinje. Miodrag Strugar *(mobile 069 02 78 82)* organises hiking tours and fishing trips and you can even spend the night at his place. His *konoba* is well-known for its excellent fish soup. Miodrag Dragojević *(mobile 067 86 01 59)* takes guests on Lake Skadar tours that include a visit to the 15th century Kom Monastery and the Skenderbeg shipwreck, that has been in the depths of Lake Skadar for 100 years. If you are there in season you can also take part in the nutmeg harvest from August to October. The villages of Staniseljići, Draževina and Gornji Kokoti are all part of the Lješanska nahija region between Podgorica, Danilovgrad and Cetinje. This has been the home of the Lješnjani clan since the 15th century. In Staniseljići, Aleksandar Bogojević *(mobile 067 53 30 01)* hosts his guests in the traditional manner in his old stone house: a slice of farm bread and some salt show as a welcome and then the table groans with all of the good things the farm and wine cellar have to offer. After your feast, you can stretch your legs by

going on a hike through the hills in the vicinity to admire the view. Old houses have been renovated and furnished in the traditional style in Draževina. Neđeljko Burzanović *(mobile 068 03 96 02)* is the owner of a wine cellar that is around 100 years old. If you want to experience real farm life, you can help him bring in the hay and even swing the scythe yourself – and, after that, stay for the night. Rajko Pejović *(mobile 067 50 98 99)* also provides accommodation in Gornji Kokoti.

After you leave Draževina or Gornji Kokoti and make your way back to the Podgorica–Danilovgrad main road and continue on for a couple of miles towards Danilovgrad and Nikšić, you will reach Bandići where Borislav Pejović *(mobile 067 53 00 39)* recounts legendary tales from the history of Montenegro. His farm is another option to overnight. The old road from Cetinje takes you to Čevo and the ham smoking operation run by Vuko Nikotić *(mobile 067 52 75 80)* in a 200-year-old house. The patron will be proud to show you his plump hams – and, of course, you will be welcome to taste them too. And, the potatoes that grow in this region are really excellent: baked in ashes and sprinkled with fresh cheese, they are delicious – and so is the home-made potato bread. Princess Jelena, King Nikola's youngest daughter – and later Queen of Italy and Albania, Empress of Ethiopia and Duchess of Savoy – was also born in this small village.

The last stage on this route takes you to the old road between Cetinje und Kotor and into the kingdom of the bees to Dubovik at the foot of the Lovćen range. Lidija Martinović *(mobile 069 67 52 71)*, whose family have been bee-keepers for many generations, produces honey, mead – old-Slavic honey wine – biscuits and cosmetics and is happy for her guests to look over her shoulder while she works.

SPORTS & ACTIVITIES

From angling to windsurfing, Montenegro offers everything a sporting enthusiast's heart desires.

It is possible to ski in some mountain valleys until July. On the other hand, hikers can already explore the north of the country on snow-free trails in April. The infrastructure in the Bjelasica, Prokletije, Durmitor and Lovćen mountain regions, as well as around Lake Skadar, has been greatly improved in recent years and tourists are now offered a choice between alpine huts, camping sites and sports clubs. The countless lakes are a paradise for bird lovers and fishermen. On the Adriatic coast tourists can relax outside in the balmy spring air from April and diving is also not a problem – if you have a wetsuit in your luggage. The Adriatic has an average temperature of over 20°C/68°F until well into September providing ideal conditions for water sports such as windsurfing, snorkelling, swimming and sailing. A rafting trip through the Tara Canyon is another very special way of enjoying the water.

ANGLING

Dozens of rivers and hundreds of brooks run through Montenegro, there are quite a few lakes including the largest one in the

Sailing, skiing, hiking and swimming in the Adriatic – there is an astonishing range of activities in this small country

Balkans – Lake Skadar – scattered throughout the country and the Adriatic also has natural fishing grounds. It is therefore no surprise that angling is almost a national sport here. Organised fish picnics on the high seas have long been a part of the standard itinerary of the tour operators on the coastal resorts. Angling trips are also offered in Virpazar on Lake Skadar. The Crno jezero lake near Žabljak and the

Morača and Lim Rivers in the highlands are especially rich in fish.

BIRD WATCHING

The variety of the Montenegro landscape ensures a wealth of birdlife that is unequalled in all of Europe. More than 300 species can be found around Lake Skadar alone, and a quarter of a million birds migrate here from the colder climes of northern Europe every winter. This is also home to pelicans and the second largest colony of cormorants in Europe. The primeval forest in the Biogradska gora National Park and the habitats in the Durmitor Mountains, where ornithologists have discovered more than 100 species to date, are also fascinating for bird lovers. The *Center for Protection and Research of Birds of Montenegro (Piperska 370a | Podgorica | mobile 067 24 50 06 | www.birdwatching mn.org)* has more detailed information.

BUNGEE JUMPING & PARAGLIDING

The coast is the realm of the daring and adventurous. There are paragliding operators in the area between Herceg Novi and Ulcinj and the two brothers Nenad and Predrag Kotlaja start their flights from Sveti Stefan. You can find more information at *www.paraglidingmontenegro. com*. Bungee jumping is offered in Budva, on Ada Bojana, at the *Spa Resort Bečići*

(Ive Lole Ribara | tel. 033 47 14 50 | www. sparesortbecici.com) in Bečići and other locations.

DIVING

Pleasant water temperatures and interesting dive sites such as coral reefs, sunken ships and underwater caves make the Adriatic ideal for divers. The water along the coast is around 35m/115ft deep and the summer temperatures are between 21–25°C/70–77°F. The dive certificates issued by the established international organisations are recognised however, it is only possible to dive with Montenegrin companies. The international database *www.dive-centers.net* offers a good overview of the local enterprises – just enter 'Montenegro' in the search field on the homepage.

MOUNTAINEERING & MOUNTAIN BIKING

An increasing number of Montenegrin

Wet fun for the adventurous: rafting in the Tara Canyon

tourists are leaving the beaches and getting out their hiking boots and bicycles to explore new territory far away from the coast. A nationwide network of cycle and hiking paths of around 6000km/3700mi has been established within the framework of the *Wilderness Hiking & Biking* project in an effort to integrate the hinterland into the country's tourist activities. Montenegro was even awarded the EcoTrophea, an international environmental prize, for this achievement. Almost all of the hiking trails lead into the fascinating landscape of the north – where there are over 150 mountains that are more than 2000m/6560ft high – to sleepy villages and cosy mountain huts. Most of the hikes are well marked with signposts.

Cyclists can choose between six national trails, ranging from easy-going to demanding, in addition to other local routes. Additional information is available on the internet under *www.montenegro.travel/en/wilderness-hiking-biking-1*. But be cautious and remember that your safety should always come first in the wild north of the country *(see p. 132)*. The mountain rescue service *(Gorska sluzba spasavanja Crne Gore | www.gss-cg.me/english)* under *tel. 040 25 60 84* or the police under *tel. 122* can help in case of an emergency.

RAFTING

A rafting tour through the deepest canyon in Europe on the Tara River is one of the highlights of any holiday in Montenegro. The river carves its way for more than 100km/62mi through the highlands, flows under the spectacular Tara Bridge – and provides lots of thrills and spills. There are tours of various lengths and a long list of operators. *Eco-Tours (Ul. Dunje Đokić | Kolašin | mobile 067 25 90 20 | www.eco-tours.co.me)* has the most comprehensive programme and, in general, accommoda-

tion options in Kolašin are usually better than in Žabljak.

SAILING

There are some well equipped marinas between Herceg Novi and Bar for Adriatic yachtsmen. The Porto Montenegro *(www.portomontenegro.com)* operation in Tivat aims to outdo Monaco and Saint Tropez. The countless regattas – mainly for small and medium-mast boats – show just how important this sport is in Montenegro. You can charter yachts and motor boats in any of the larger towns on the coast. Podgorica is also the headquarter of the *Montenegro Charter Company (Bulevar Svetog Petra Cetinjskog 92 | tel. 020 22 95 85 | www.montenegrocharter.com)*

SKIING

The continental climate in the north guarantees freezing winters in the Montenegro's mountains. The two ski centres of Durmitor and Bjelasica are especially popular with winter sport enthusiasts from the former Yugoslavian republics from December through to March. The hotels in Kolašin organise transfers to the slopes in the *Bjelasic* ski centre 8km/5mi away. The offer in the Žabljak area is even more varied: *Savin kuk, Štuoc* and *Javoravaca* are the ski slopes in the Durmitor Mountains that are over 2000m/6560ft in places.

WINDSURFING

Experienced windsurfers will be delighted by the high waves and strong winds off the coast near Ulcinj. Beginners, on the other hand, should enjoy the protected waters of the Bay of Kotor. It is also fun to try the fresh-water variety: people have recently started windsurfing on Lake Skadar once again.

TRAVEL WITH KIDS

There is a Montenegrin saying that children are the happiness of the world. They take an active part in family life and are often allowed to stay up very late. And the offspring of foreign guests are also usually free to do as they please. So if properly planned, this country can be a paradise for children. There are slides and swings in many of the parks – but you take care as they are not all in the best condition – and they can have a lot of fun on the water slides and pedal boats that can be found at almost every beach. The boat tours that are available all along the coast are a special treat, and for the really adventurous there are dive courses especially for children. This is not common practice in Montenegro but restaurants are usually happy to oblige if requested. Take care on the roads and paths because they frequently lack pavements.

BAY OF KOTOR

The international children's carnival is held in June every year in Herceg Novi (122 C5) (*ω H5*) and the colourful splendour of the summer carnival in Kotor (123 E–F 4–5) (*ω K5*) in August will really delight the little ones. A unique sight is the Fašinada in July *(www.visit-montenegro.com/cities-kotor.htm)*, a procession on the water when rowing boats with torches make their way from Perast (123 D–E4) (*ω J4*) to the small island of Gospa od Škrpjela.

THE ADRIATIC

A 80,000ft² large *Aquapark (adults 15, children 10 euros)*, the most attractive in Montenegro, is part of the *Mediteran (230 rooms | tel. 033 42 40 00 | www.hotel mediteran.info | Expensive)* hotel complex in Bečići (124 C5) (*ω M6*). There are two swimming pools especially for children. Holidaymakers who go to the Adriatic with their offspring in November – it is often still possible to swim then – can visit the *Susreti pod starom maslinom* exhibition near Bar (126 A–B 4–5) (*ω P7*). Children display their works on the theme of 'Olive, Peace, Friendship' under the oldest olive tree in the country. Children can learn to ride on the Grand Beach in Ulcinj (127 D6) (*ω R8*). Riding lessons can

Horseback riding on the beach, petting animals on a farm, diving in the Adriatic – Montenegro offers a great deal to young visitors

be booked locally at the hotels that are members of the *Ulcinjska rivijera (www.ulcinjska-rivijera.com/eng)* association.

CETINJE, PODGORICA & LAKE SKADAR

The life and work of Montenegro's poet Prince Njegoš in Cetinje (124 C3–4) (*ill* L–M4) are on display for both adults and children at the *Biljarda* which also houses the gigantic INSIDER TIP three-dimensional relief map of Montenegro *(entrance fee Biljarda 3 euros, relief map 1 euro extra)* in the southern section of the museum courtyard. The bird's-eye views affords a completely new, fascinating perspective.

THE NORTH-WEST

The pristine Durmitor (120–121 B–D 2–3)

(*ill* U–W 11–12) still has farms where goat and sheep milk cheese is made by hand from the milk of free-range animals. Ask locally where you can find a *katun*. The proverbially hospitable Montenegrins will let the children play with their animals and show them how they make cheese.

THE NORTH-EAST

A small INSIDER TIP botanical garden *(Botanička Bašta | Dulovina near Kolašin* (121 D4) *(ill* W13) *| telephonic appointments necessary | mobile: 069 01 54 78 | entrance fee 2 euros)* is the life's work of the 'herb king' of Montenegro, Daniel Vincek, who also makes medicinal teas out of his herbs. There is a fine exhibition of mountain flora and Mr Vincek is a very friendly person who will be happy to answer any questions.

FESTIVALS & EVENTS

FESTIVALS & EVENTS

JANUARY

A rather different Christmas with pagan church rituals, Orthodox choirs and colourful processions. ▶ ● *Christmas Eve* on 6 Jan is a very special event that is celebrated with much pomp in the churches and monasteries. An oak branch, the *badnjak*, brought into the house brings luck

FEBRUARY

▶ *Mimosa Festival* in Herceg Novi. The first mimosa blossoms are greeted with fanfare on the waterfront promenade. During the ▶ INSIDER TIP *carnival period* there are masked balls and colourful processions along the coast in Kotor and many other places

MARCH

▶ *In the footsteps of King Nikola:* international multi-stage bicycle race through mountains and valleys

APRIL

▶ *Palm Sunday (Vrbica)* is a special day for children in the Orthodox Church. People make wreathes out of palm fronds, a little bell rings and the priests bless the processions with incense as they make their way around the church
▶ *Jazz at Noon* is the motto on 30 April when the International Jazz Day is celebrated in ten large towns including Podgorica, Budva and Kotor

MAY

Free climbers shin up the steep cliffs in Kotor and Nikšić in their attempts to win the ▶ *Montenegro Cup*
The ▶ *Night of the Museums* is celebrated throughout the country on 19 May
▶ *Tito's Birthday* is celebrated on 25 May in Tivat with flags and revolutionary songs

The first spring festival starts just after Christmas, and carnival comes twice a year – there are plenty of celebrations in Montenegro

JULY

▶ *Fashion Week* in Kotor shows Dior and Gucci along with creations by local Montenegrin designers

▶ INSIDER TIP *Festival of Male Choirs* in Perast. The *klape* have no more than eight members and perform their repertoire a capella

▶ *Bridge Diving* in Mojkovac: the brave are awarded prizes for jumping into the river from the Tara Bridge

AUGUST

Films from the region compete for the Golden Mimosa at the ▶ INSIDER TIP *Montenegro Film Festival* held at the beginning of the month in the Turkish fortress Kanli kula in Herceg Novi. Although not all of the films are shown with English subtitles, the screenings in the open air are always a great experience. Expert collectors show everything that grows in the area at the

▶ *Mushroom and Herb Fair* in Rožaje

▶ *Swimming Marathon* along the coast between Bar and Sutomore

▶ INSIDER TIP *Summer Carnival* in Kotor and Petrovac

SEPTEMBER

▶ *Food Fair* in Virpazar: wine estates, fruit farmers and bee-keepers present their products. There is also dancing and singing

OCTOBER

▶ *Halloween* in Budva: witches and elves take over for one day

DECEMBER

There are free open air ▶ *New Year's concerts* and fireworks displays in many towns and cities just before midnight on 31 Dec. And, of course, there simply has to be a fireworks display

LINKS, BLOGS, APPS & MORE

LINKS

▶ www.bestof-montenegro.com An excellent resource on Montenegro that offers a great deal of information with numerous categories covering hotels, beaches, restaurants and attractions. The site also has a link to the official tourist site

▶ www.discover-montenegro.com Information on the culture and history, geography and nature, of Montenegro as well as tips for various activities and many photos

▶ www.montenegro-mountains.com/zabljak-durmitor This excellent website is devoted to the mountainous Durmitor region in the north-west. There are lovely photographs and a video along with informative texts on culture and nature and activities that can be carried out during the various seasons.

▶ www.visit-montenegro.com All you need to know about your destination at a glance: interactive maps with planning function, a link to a video channel with videos about Montenegro, online booking services and much more

BLOGS & FORUMS

▶ www.montenegro-forum.com Montenegro visitors exchange information on all aspects of travel in the country. You will find general tourist tips as well as articles on the different regions Montenegro, individual towns and villages and the national parks

▶ lifeinmontenegro.com A Canadian now living in Montenegro dishes the scoop on where to find the best restaurants and bars, and writes about his recent trips and other local adventures

▶ short.travel/mon2 Very informative, English-language forum. Here you will find information on the entire region but there is always a link to Montenegro

Regardless of whether you are still preparing your trip or already in Montenegro: these addresses will provide you with more information, videos and networks to make your holiday even more enjoyable

VIDEOS

▶ www.montenegro.travel/en/multimedia/video-galerija A link to a wide selection of travel documentaries showing impressions of the country including mountain biking, hiking, national parks and many other locations

▶ www.visit-montenegro.tv/related-videos/tara-rafting A six minute travel report that gives you an idea of what to expect from a rafting trip on the Tara

▶ short.travel/mon5 The film on the Durmitor National Park is part of the Traveline series of travel documentaries. Three clips on the Bay of Kotor, Lake Skadar and the train ride through the Morača Canyon on the way from Bar to Belgrade can also be seen on their YouTube channel

▶ www.youtube.com/watch?v=QSxOWCiDzDE Rambo Amadeus, Montenegro's 'Frank Zappa' was his country's representative at the 2012 Eurovision Song Contest. He only came 15th but his song 'Euro – Neuro' makes fun of the power of money in everyday life and provides a witty commentary on the European currency

APPS

▶ Explore Montenegro This app for Android smartphones is a helpful travel companion with an overview of the most important tourist destinations and cultural and historical information

▶ Montenegro Video Travel Guide This app will whet your appetite for your holiday in Montenegro with more than 35 minutes of filmed material and many photos, for all smartphones and tablets

NETWORK

▶ www.facebook.com/budva This Facebook site does not only show pictures of Budva but all Montenegro. Interesting links and videos are also posted here

▶ www.couchsurfing.org Members of this hospitable community offer free accommodation visitors to Montenegro

▶ Airbnb Is a popular site for tourists who prefer to stay in private accommodation offered by locals. A search under Montenegro pulls up the full spectrum from a quaint apartment in the old town section of Budva to a stone house in the mountains

TRAVEL TIPS

ARRIVAL

🚗 If you drive, you can either take the E65 coastal road via Slovenia and Croatia to Montenegro or the E45/E55 to the Italian ports of Bari or Ancona via Austria and Switzerland. Car ferries *(www.montenegrolines.net)* depart from there to Bar on the other side of the Adriatic. The trip from Bari takes nine to ten hours and a place on deck costs around 48 euros in season; a simple cabin costs 80–100 euros and it is about 78 euros per car. The crossing from Ancona takes about 16 hours and is somewhat more expensive.

🚂 Trains depart from several destinations in Europe for Belgrade; this is the unavoidable stopover before travelling on to Montenegro. You then continue on via Bijelo Polje, Mojkovac, Kolašin and Podgorica to Bar on the Adriatic. The landscape along this route is one of the most impressive in the Balkans and more than compensates for the stress of the twelve hour train ride.

🚌 There is a well developed bus network linking Montenegro to Europe via Dubrovnik or Belgrade.

✈ Montenegro Airlines *(www.monte negroairlines.com)* flies to Tivat and Podgorica from several European destinations. Air Serbia (formerly Jat Airways) serves numerous international destinations from Belgrade with connecting flights to Tivat and Podgorica. It is also possible to fly to Dubrovnik and then take a taxi to your destination in Montenegro: the trip to Budva (90km/56mi) costs around 80 euros, to Herceg Novi (20km/12.5mi) around 30 euros.

BANKS & CREDIT CARDS

There are banks and ATMs on almost every corner in the towns on the coast. However, if you travel into the mountains, you should be sure to take some cash with you. The daily limit for withdrawals from a cash dispenser is 700 euros. Hotels and supermarkets accept the standard credit cards but you should ask beforehand in restaurants and small shops.

CAMPING

Camping sites are known as *kampovi* or *auto kampovi* in Montenegro. They are popular and well equipped on the coast and in the mountains. You can find good descriptions of all the sites under *http://en.camping.info/campsites* search 'Montenegro'.

RESPONSIBLE TRAVEL

It doesn't take a lot to be environmentally friendly whilst travelling. Don't just think about your carbon footprint whilst flying to and from your holiday destination but also about how you can protect nature and culture abroad. As a tourist it is especially important to respect nature, look out for local products, cycle instead of driving, save water and much more. If you would like to find out more about eco-tourism please visit: *www.ecotourism.org*

Holiday from start to finish: the most important addresses and information for your trip to Montenegro

It can be quite loud at night in the establishments on the promenade or in the old parts of town (such as in Budva or Kotor).

CONSULATES & EMBASSIES

BRITISH EMBASSY
Ulcinjska 8| Podgorica | tel. +382 20 61 80 10 | ukinmontenegro.fco.gov.uk/en

UNITED STATES EMBASSY
Dzona Dzeksona 2 | Podgorica | tel. +382 020 41 05 07 | podgorica.usembassy.gov

CUSTOMS

It is permitted to bring currency up to an amount of 10,000 euros into or out of the country. It is prohibited to import food with the exception of dried fruit, tea and coffee, 2L of juice and 5L of water. In addition, 2L of alcohol up to 22 per cent or 1L of spirits over 22 per cent and 200 cigarettes or 50 cigars can be imported duty free. The same amounts of alcohol and tobacco goods can be taken back into the EU.

DRIVING

National registration papers and driving licenses are recognised. It is obligatory to have a green international insurance card and you will need to show it at the border when you enter the country. Maximum speed limits: in built up areas 40km/h, on country roads 80km/h, on motorways 100km/h. Vehicles with trailers are not allowed to exceed 80km/h.
Traffic fines are heavy: overtake in a tunnel or run a red light and you will lose your license; telephoning in the car – 20 euros; driving without wearing a seat-

BUDGETING

Ice cream	£0.80/$1.30
	for one scoop
Snack	£1.50/$2
	for a slice of pizza
Coffee	£0.80–1.50/$1.30–2.60
	for an espresso
Petrol	£1.15/$1.8
	for 1 litre of super
Bus ticket	£2/$3.5
	for a trip from Budva to Petrovac (about 20km/12.5mi)
Boat tour	£8–33/$13–52
	for a fish picnic on the Adriatic Meer

belt – 15 euros. You should contact the police immediately if you have an accident. The emergency service *(tel. 198 07)* will provide assistance if you have a breakdown on the road. The parking fees are extremely high on the coast – up to 15 euros a day – and there is usually no guarantee given for the safety of your car. International and national car hire agencies have branches in most of the major holiday resorts. Travel agencies will also take care of bookings. It is usually less expensive to hire a car at your destination than to book one through the major organisations such as Avis or Europcar. Be sure to check the prices and service as some companies charge additional amounts for taxes and insurance. The price for a small car such as a Renault Clio, Fiat Panda or Opel Corsa is around 200 euros for 7 days and from 47 euros a day for larger vehicles.

CURRENCY CONVERTER

£	€	€	£
1	1.20	1	0.85
3	3.60	3	2.55
5	6	5	4.25
13	15.60	13	11
40	48	40	34
75	90	75	64
120	144	120	100
250	300	250	210
500	600	500	425

$	€	€	$
1	0.75	1	1.30
3	2.30	3	3.90
5	3.80	5	6.50
13	10	13	17
40	30	40	50
75	55	75	97
120	90	120	155
250	185	250	325
500	370	500	650

For current exchange rates see www.xe.com

EMERGENCY SERVICES

Police *tel. 122,* fire brigade *tel. 123,* and emergency doctor *tel. 124.* Include the country code *+382* if you do not have a Montenegrin SIM card.

HEALTH

There are state-run clinics in almost every town or village, they are marked with a red cross. You will have to pay for any treatment you receive and it is therefore a good idea to have foreign travel health insurance with the option of repatriation. Private clinics have been established in the larger towns. The local tourist office can give you the addresses of local doctors – most of them speak English. The well-stocked pharmacies can provide help for minor mishaps.

IMMIGRATION

Visas are not required for those arriving from the EU, Australia, New Zealand, Canada and the US. An identity card is sufficient if you do not plan to be in the country for longer than 30 days but a passport is required for stays of up to 90 days. Tourists from other countries will need a passport and should check with their travel agents what other requirements need to be fulfilled. The visitors' tax is 1 euro per day and is usually included in the price of accommodation. In addition, each tourist has to be registered with the police. As a rule, the person who provides your accommodation takes care of this and will ask you for your ID or passport when you check in. Remember to take your registration certificate with you when you leave the country – it is sometimes asked for at the border!

INFORMATION

NACIONALNA TURISTIČKA ORGANIZACIJA CRNE GORE (NTO)
Bulevar Svetog Petra Cetinjskog 130 | Podgorica | tel. 077 10 00 01 | 24 hour information telephone 13 00 | www.monte negro.travel
The National Tourist Organisation of Montenegro (NTO) has branches throughout the country and there are travel agencies in almost every town.
The official website of the NTO *www.mon tenegro.travel* provides detailed information on the internet. The *www.bestof montenegro.com*, with a list of the best beaches, hotels and restaurants, is another helpful site.

INTERNET & WI-FI

Almost all the hotels have wireless connections – and so do most private accommodation and camping sites. Cafés have notices up if they have a Wi-Fi hotspot and some restaurants and pubs provide internet access. As a rule the larger the town, the better the internet connection. If you decide to travel with your laptop and want to use it where there is no Wi-Fi, you can buy internet cards at any post office. The cheapest cost 10 euros but they do not last long.

NUDISTS

There are limited options for nude bathing in Montenegro. The official nudist beach on Ada Bojana near Ulcinj is restricted to guests living in the complex. A small rock is reserved for naturists in Ulcinj itself. The small Nijivce nudist beach is located at the outermost tip of Igalo.

Fishing boats take tourists from other resorts to small bays where they can bathe nude. Ask on the site!

OPENING HOURS

There are no fixed opening hours in Montenegro and some shops and restaurants stay open until midnight in summer. Many offices close at 4pm. Post offices are open from 7am–8pm on weekdays and sometimes longer during the tourist season.

PHONES & MOBILE PHONES

Montenegro has more mobile phones than inhabitants and it therefore comes as no surprise that three mobile phone providers vie for their customers: Telenor *(069)*, m:tel *(068)* und T-Com *(067)*. All three also provide mobile internet. The prices per minute are higher than elsewhere in Europe and international roaming

BOOKS & FILMS

▶ **Encyclopaedia of the Dead** – Danilo Kiš (1935–89) is considered to be one of the most important writers in the Balkans. His parables on life, love and death made him famous and most of his books have been published in English.

▶ **Bridge over the Drina** – In 1961, Ivo Andrić (1892–1975) won the Nobel Prize for Literature for his story about the stone bridge that was built over the Drina River during the Turkish era. The author spent the last years of his life in Herceg Novi.

▶ **The New Class** – The main work by Milovan Đilas (Djilas) (1911–95) is a

scathing indictment of Socialism in the former Yugoslavia. Many of the other books by the former Montenegrin partisan, who later became a dissident in Tito's Yugoslavia, have been translated into English.

▶ **The Battle of Neretva** – This film (1969) is one of the several the director Veljko Bulajić made in the 1960s that deals with the struggles of the Yugoslav partisans against the German army in the Second World War. The productions were heavily subsidised by the Yugoslav state. The stars include Orson Welles and Yul Brynner.

Take care on the roads here

An extensive bus network connects all of the major cities in Montenegro with each other and there are also several lines that travel regularly between the main destinations on the coast. Tickets can be purchased at the bus terminals *(autobuska stanica)* or from the driver and are very inexpensive when compared with the tariffs in the rest of Europe. The train from Bar to Belgrade makes several stops in Sutomore, Podgorica, Kolašin, Mojkovac and Bijelo Polje every day.

charges are also rather steep. If you intend to use your mobile phone in Montenegro, it is a good idea to buy a prepaid card with a Montenegrin number which can be had for as little as 5 euros from any newspaper kiosk. Telephone cards for fixed-line connections are available from post offices.

The dialling code for Montenegro is *+382* followed by the area code. International dialling codes: United Kingdom *+44*, Australia *+61*, Canada and USA *+1*, Ireland *+353*.

TIME

Macedonia has Central European Time (or Central European Summer Time) and is one hour ahead of GMT.

TIPPING

It is customary to round up small amounts in cafés. However, tourists should leave a tip of 10–15 per cent of bill.

PRICES

Prices for food have increased by almost 50 per cent in recent years. Sausage and cheese, for example, are only slightly less expensive than in many European countries. The same applies to fruit and vegetables that are not imported. And, prices vary throughout the country: for example, many products are cheaper in Bar than in Budva. As a rule, life in the interior is cheaper than on the coast. The sun loungers you hire on the beaches can also be expensive. It is common to pay around 10 euros and if you want to live in grand style, you can pay up to 100 euros for a bed shaded by a canopy on the beach.

WHEN TO GO

In July and Aug when the temperatures on the coast can soar to 40°C/104°F – and even higher in the valley around Podgorica – it is still a temperate 20°C/68°F in the Durmitor mountains. Winters are mild on the coast and harsh in the mountains. The best months for a beach holiday are May/June and Sept/Oct. The extreme heat and overcrowded beaches in the school holiday months of July and August can make a holiday rather stressful during that period. The water temperature is more than 20°C/68°F by June and this can reach 29°C/84°F at the end of the season. There is a good deal of snow in the mountains between Dec and March and it is even possible to ski in some places in summer.

WHERE TO STAY

The days of simply furnished rooms *(sobe)* on the coast have come to an end but they are still offered in the mountains where nature-loving tourists will find more rustic accommodation. Elegant hotels are now shooting up all along the Adriatic.

This building boom has also reached the owners of private houses. Apartments *(apartmani)* can be found on every corner. Internet and cable TV have become standard features and there is often even a view of the sea – if there is no construction going on right in front of your window! There is a great difference in the prices charged on the coast: Herceg Novi, Budva and Perast are the most expensive and things start to become cheaper after you leave Petrovac and head towards Ulcinj. An overnight stay in an apartment in Ulcinj costs only 3–6 euros in the season, while it is not possible to find anything under 10–15 euros in Budva at the same time. The prices often fall by up to 40 per cent in the off peak seasons. You will be able to find countless offers if you do an internet search. But while it is easy to read the addresses on the internet because they are in Latin letters but it becomes more difficult when you are actually in the country. All of the street names are written in Cyrillic letters – you will just have to ask the way.

WEATHER IN BUDVA

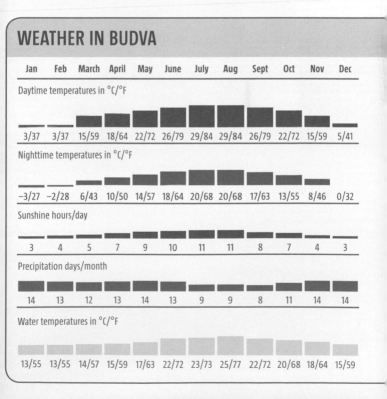

	Jan	Feb	March	April	May	June	July	Aug	Sept	Oct	Nov	Dec
Daytime temperatures in °C/°F	3/37	3/37	15/59	18/64	22/72	26/79	29/84	29/84	26/79	22/72	15/59	5/41
Nighttime temperatures in °C/°F	−3/27	−2/28	6/43	10/50	14/57	18/64	20/68	20/68	17/63	13/55	8/46	0/32
Sunshine hours/day	3	4	5	7	9	10	11	11	8	7	4	3
Precipitation days/month	14	13	12	13	14	13	9	9	8	11	14	14
Water temperatures in °C/°F	13/55	13/55	14/57	15/59	17/63	22/72	23/73	25/77	22/72	20/68	18/64	15/59

USEFUL PHRASES MONTENEGRIN

PRONUNCIATION

As a general rule, Montenegrin is pronounced as it is written. Special Montenegrin letters and combinations:

c – ts as in ca**ts**; **č** – ch as in **ch**urch; **ć** –ch as in fu**t**ure; **đ** – j as in **j**ungle; **dž** – j as in a**dj**acent; **j** – y as in **y**outh; **lj** – li as in mi**lli**on; **nj** – ny as in ca**ny**on; **š** – sh as in **sh**ip; **ž** – s as in plea**s**ure.

All vowels are open and must be clearly voiced regardless of their position. In vowel combinations each vowel is audible, as in petnaest = pet-na-est (fifteeen). Similarly, the r which plays the role of the syllable nucleus in certain words, must also be clearly voiced: vrba, krk.

The consonants are always pronounced the same, e.g. the **g** as in **g**one is always the hard g.

Abbreviation: *f* = female speaker

IN BRIEF

Yes/No/Maybe	da/ne/možda
Please/Thank you	molim/hvala
Excuse me, please!	Oprostite (Izvinite)!
May I ...?	Da li mogu ...?
Pardon?	Molim?
I would like to .../have you got ...?	Želim .../Da li imate?
How much is ...?	Koliko košta?
I (don't) like this.	To mi se (ne) sviđa.
good/bad	dobro/loše
broken/does't work	nije ispravno
too much/much/little	previše/mnogo/malo
all/nothing	sve/ništa
Help!/Attention!/Caution!	Upomoć!/Pažnja!/Oprez!
ambulance/police/fire brigade	ambulantna kola/policija/vatrogasci
Prohibition/forbidden	zabrana/zabranjeno
danger/dangerous	opasnost/opasno
May I take a photo of you?	Da li smem da Vas fotografišem?

GREETINGS, FAREWELL

Good morning!/afternoon!/ evening!/night!	Dobro jutro!/Dobar dan!/ Dobro veče!/Laku noć!

GOVORIŠ LI CRNOGORSKI?

"Do you speak Montenegrin?" This guide will help you to say the basic words and phrases in Montenegrin

Hello! / Goodbye!/See you!	Zdravo!/Doviđenja!
Bye!	Zdravo!/Ciao!
My name is ...	Zovem se ...
What's your name?	Kako se zovete/zoveš?
I'm from ...	Dolazim iz ...

DATE & TIME

Monday/Tuesday/Wednesday	ponedjeljak/utorak/srijeda
Thursday/Friday/Saturday	četvrtak/petak/subota
Sunday/holiday/	nedjelja/praznik
today/tomorrow/yesterday	danas/sjutra/juče
hour/minute	sat/minuta
day/night/week/month/year	dan/noć/sedmica/mjesec/godina
What time is it?	Je sati?
It's three o'clock.	Tri sata je.
It's half past three.	Tri i po.
a quarter to four.	petnaest do četiri.
a quarter past four.	četiri i petnaest minuta.

TRAVEL

open/closed	otvoreno/zatvoreno
entrance/exit	ulaz/izlaz
departure/arrival	odlazak/polijetanje / dolazak
toilets/ladies/gentlemen	WC, toalet/žene/muškarci
(no) drinking water	(nije) pijaća voda
Where is ...?/Where are ...?	Gdje je ...?/Gdje su ...?
left/right/straight ahead/back	lijevo/desno/pravo/nazad
close/far	blizu/daleko
bus/tram/underground/taxi (cab)	autobus/tramvaj/metro/taksi
stop/taxi (cab) stand	stajalište/taksi-stanica
parking lot/parking garage	parking/parking garaža
street map/map	plan grada/geografska (auto-)karta
train station/harbour/airport	željeznička stanica/luka/aerodrom
schedule/ticket	red vožnje/biljet, karta
single/return/supplement	jednostavno/tamo i nazad/doplata
train/track/platform	voz/kolosek/peron
I would like to rent ...	Htio (f htjela) bih ... da iznajmim.
a car/a bicycle/a boat	auto/bicikl/čamac
petrol/gas station / petrol/gas / diesel	benzinska pumpa/benzin/dizel
breakdown/repair shop	kvar/automehaničarska radionica

FOOD & DRINK

Could you please book a table for tonight for four?	Molim vas rezervaciju za večeras jedan sto za četiri osobe.
on the terrace/by the window	na terasi/pored prozora
The menu, please.	Jelovnik, (meni) molim.
Could I please have ...?	Molim vas, htio (f htjela) bih ...?
bottle/carafe/glass	bocu/bokal/čašu
knife/fork/spoon	nož/viljušku/kašiku
salt/pepper/sugar/vinegar/oil	so/biber/šećer/sirće/ulje
milk/cream/lemon	mlijeko/skorup/limun
with/without ice	sa/bez leda
sparkling/non-sparkling	gazirana/negazirana
vegetarian/allergy	vegetarijanac (f vegetarijanka)/alergija
May I have the bill, please?	Molim vas, htio (f htjela) bih da platim.
bill/receipt/tip	račun/priznanica/bakšiš

SHOPPING

Where can I find...?	Gdje mogu naći?
I'd like .../I'm looking for ...	Htio (f htjela) bih .../Tražim ...
baker/market/grocery	pekara/pijaca/tržnica
shopping centre/department store	šoping mol/robna kuća
supermarket/newspaper shop/kiosk	supermarket/trafika/kiosk
100 grammes/1 kilo	sto grama/jedan kilogram
expensive/cheap/price	skupo/jetino/cijena
more/less	više/manje
organically grown	organska hrana

ACCOMMODATION

I have booked a room.	Rezervisao sam jednu sobu.
Do you have any ... left?	Da li imate još ...?
single room/double room	jednokrevetnu sobu/dvokrevetnu sobu
breakfast/half board/full board (American plan)	doručak/polupansion/puni pansion
at the front/seafront/lakefront	napried/prema moru/prema jezeru
shower/sit-down bath/balcony/terrace	tuš/kupatilo/balkon/terasa
key/room card	ključevi/elektronska karta za sobu
luggage/suitcase/bag	prtljag/kufer/torba

BANKS, MONEY & CREDIT CARDS

bank/ATM/pin code	banka/bankovni automat/lični broj
cash/credit card	keš/kreditna kartica
bill/coin/change	novčanica/metalni novac/kusur

HEALTH

doctor/dentist/paediatrician	ljekar/zubar/dječji ljekar, pedijatar
hospital/emergency clinic/pharmacy	bolnica/urgentni centar/apoteka
fever/pain	groznica/bolovi
diarrhoea/nausea	proliv, dijareja/mučnina
sunburn	opekotine od sunca
inflamed/injured	upala, infekcija/povrijeđen
plaster/bandage	flaster/zavoj
pain reliever/tablet/suppository	analgetik/tableta/čepići

POST, TELECOMMUNICATIONS & MEDIA

stamp/letter/postcard	poštanska marka/pismo/razglednica
I need a landline phone card.	Treba mi jedna telefonska kartica za fiksni telefon.
I'm looking for a prepaid card for my mobile.	Tražim jednu pripejd-karticu za mobilni telefon.
Where can I find internet access?	Gdje ću naći internet-vezu?
internet connection/wi-fi	utičnica za internet/WLAN

LEISURE, SPORTS & BEACH

beach/bathing beach	plaža/kupalište
sunshade/lounger	suncobran/ležaljka
low tide/high tide/current	osjeka/plima/struja
cable car/chair lift	žičara/ski-lift
(rescue) hut/avalanche	planinska brvnara/lavina

NUMBERS

0	nula	15	petnaest
1	jedan (f jedna, n jedno)	16	šesnaest
2	dva (f dvije)	17	sedamnaest
3	tri	18	osamnaest
4	četiri	19	devetnaest
5	pet	70	sedamdeset
6	šest	80	osamdeset
7	sedam	90	devedeset
8	osam	100	sto, stotina
9	devet	200	dvjesta
10	deset	1000	hiljadu
11	jedanaest	2000	dvije hiljade
12	dvanaest	10000	deset hiljada
13	trinaest	½	polovina
14	četrnaest	¼	četvrtina

NOTES

FOR YOUR NEXT HOLIDAY ...

MARCO POLO TRAVEL GUIDES

- PACKED WITH INSIDER TIPS
- BEST WALKS AND TOURS
- FULL-COLOUR PULL-OUT MAP
  AND STREET ATLAS

ROAD ATLAS

The green line ▭ indicates the Trips & Tours (p. 90–95)
The blue line ▭ indicates The perfect route (p. 30–31)

All tours are also marked on the pull-out map

Photo: The Bay of Kotor

Exploring Montenegro

The map on the back cover shows how the area has been sub-divided

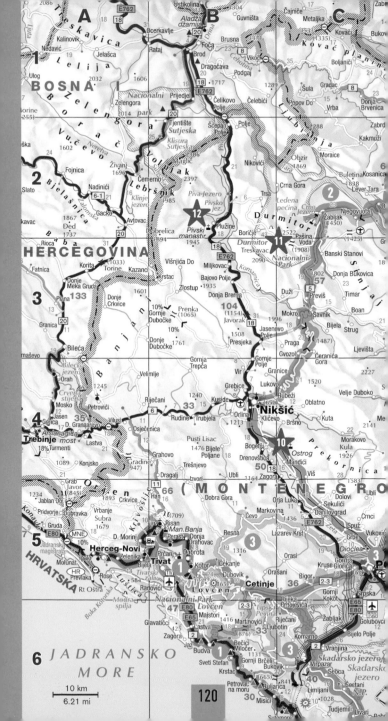

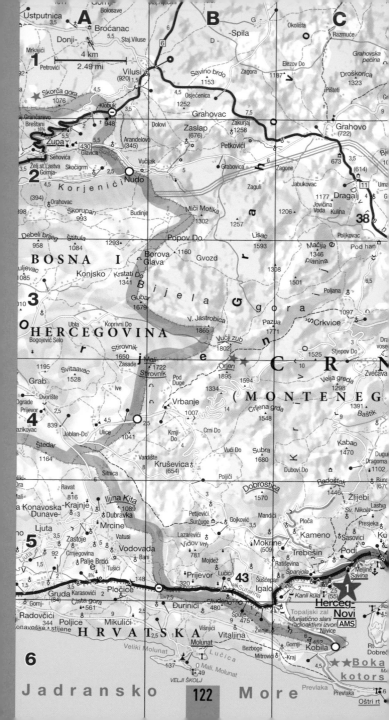

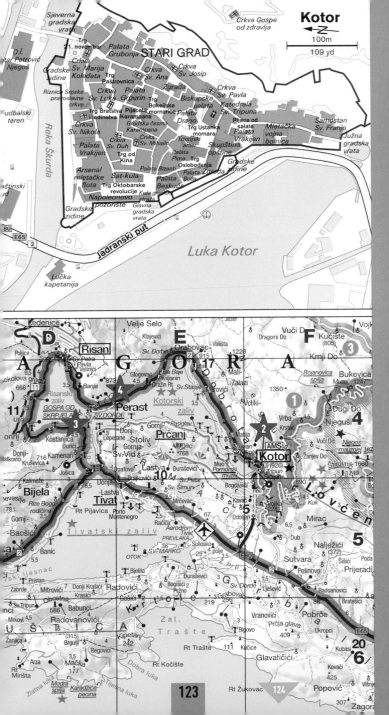

Kotor

100m
109 yd

STARI GRAD

Sjeverna gradska vrata
Crkva Gospe od zdravlja
Trg 21. novembar
Palata Grubonja
O.I. Petrović Njegoš
Gradske zidine
Sv. Marija Koledata
Riznici Srpske pravoslavne crkve
Crkva Sv. Luka
Trg Paštrovnica
Crkva Sv. Ana
Crkva Sv. Josip
Palata Grgurin
Crkva Sv. Pavla
Zgrada
Biskupska palata
Katedrala Sv. Tripuna
Trg Bratstva jedinstva
Palata Bokeljske mornarice
Trg Karampana
Pijaca mornarice
Palata Drago
Trg Ustanka mornara
Pjaca od salata
Palata Vrakijen
Samostan Sv. Franjo
Mletačka vojna bolnica
Crkva Sv. Nikola
Gradska česma Karampana
Crkva Sv. Duh
Crkva Sv. Mihailo
Istorijski arhiv
Skupština opštine
Palata Vrakijen
Palata od Kina
Palata Pima
Trg Oslobođenja
Palata Bizanti
Palata Buća
Zgrada Beskuća
Gradske zidine
Arsenal mletačke flote
Sat-kula
Trg Oktobarske revolucije
Kula gradske straže
Napoleonovo pozorište
Glavna gradska vrata
Gradske zidine
Udbalski teren
Reka Škurda
E65
2
80
Jadranski put
Lučka kapetanija

Luka Kotor

Ledenice
Velje Selo
Jezer
Vuči D
Kučište (805)
Vojk
Police
D
Risan
G
Klajevići
Sv. Đorđe
E
Orahovac
915
1228
Vališta
Dragomi Do
F
3
Krnji Do
A
G
O
R
A
Sokolova greda
9,5
11
666
Sv. Petra
Sv. Pavla
Veliniči
3,5
Banja
Glogovac
873
Kula Baje
Pivljanin
Dražin Rt
Nuta
Mali-Zalazi
Sv.Stasje
Vučiki.
1350
Bojanovica spilja
Muzej 1247
Bukovica
14½
Dugi Do
Njeguši
4
11
Ligi
Risanski zaliv
GOSPA OD SKRPJELA
SV.ĐORĐE
4
Perast
Kotorski zaliv
3,5
Vrba
Krstac
4,5
3
Kostanjica
Đurići
716 Kamenari
Donji-latkovici
Donji-
Kruševica
Jošica
Donji
Lepetane
Gornji
Stoliv
Sv.Vid
Opatovo
3
Prčanj
Donji
Sv. Matija
Vrmac
768
Sv.Ivan
Sv.Nikola
AMS
Kotor
5 (926)
Sv Tripun
Njegoš mauzolej Jez
Žanjev Do
Vuči Do
Strovnik 1660
1749
L
o
v
č
e
n
Kalimože
Lastva
Đuraševići
Pomorski muzej
Muo
Bijela
781
Rize Bog
rodična
3,5
Donja-
Lastva
Sv. Petar
Sv. Šimun
Brajkovići
10
Mrčevac
Bogdašići
Gornji-
Baošići
Tivat
Rt Pijavica
Porto Montenegro
Kavač
2,5
Račica
67
Odoljin
Trojica 228
Kuk
890
4,5
Mirac
5
Banic
Tivatski zaliv
Aerodrom Tivat
PREVLAKA
polje
E80
6,5
Dub
Naljezići (372)
5
ski ljesnac
OTOK
SV. MARKO
Soliosko
3,5
zup
2
Sutvara
Pelinovo
Šišići
Prijeradi
Poda
Pristan
Zabrde
Bjelila
Đuraševići
36
29
Sv. Đorđe
G
Lješević
Radanović
Brateš
Mitrovići
Donji Krašići
Radovići
Bogišići 2
Pržno
Grabova
256
Sv.Tripun
586
Obostnik
Krasići
Gošići
219
Vranovići
Pobrđe
E65
nci
Mrkovi
Babunci
Ko
Zal.
Prčja glava
409
Ukropci
20
U
Š
Radovanovići
C
A
Trašte
Bigovo
6
Zanjica
(315)
Brguli
Kipetan
242
Begovići
Glavatičići
Kubasi
6
Arza
Rt Mirišta
Mačka
177
3,5
Dobra luka
Rt Trašte
111
Kučiče
Kovači
425
Višnje
Modra spilja
Karadžica pecina
Tijesna luka
Rt Kočište
Rt Žukovac
Popović
307
Zlatna luka
Zagora

124

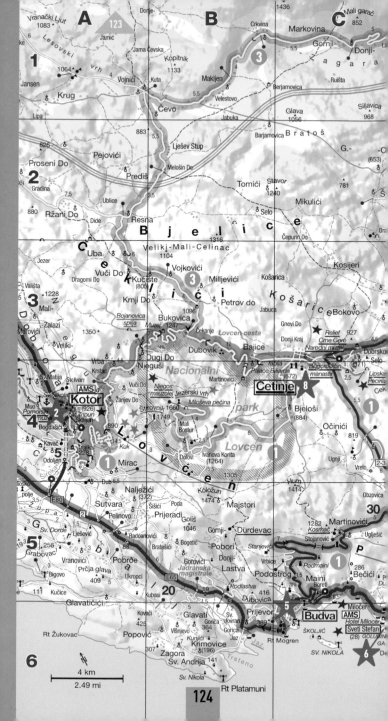

A   B   C

Vranački Ljut
1083

Jamić

Lesovski vrh

1064

Jansen

Krug

Vojnići

Kuta

Kopitnik
1133

Dorje-

Crkvina

Markovina

Mali garač
852

Gornji-

Donji-

agara

Ruišta

Siljavica
968

Lipa

Cevo

Makljen

5.5

Velestovo

Berjamovica

Glava
1056

1436

Ruišta

Proseni Do

Gradina

7.5

Pejovići

Prediš

Melošin Do

Lješev Stup

Barjamovica

Tomići

Stavor
1240

Bratoš

G.-

(653)

-C

781

Š

825

880

Ržani Do

Dide

Ublice

Resna

Selo

Mikulići

Selo

1316

Čepurin Do

Ori-

B j e l i c e

Jezer

Vališta

1228

Mali-

Zalazi

Doblo

Marovići

1350

Veliki-

Uba

Vuči Do

Dragomi Do

Kučište
(805)

Krnji Do

Veliki-Mali-Celinac
1104

Vojkovići

Millijevići

1096

Petrov do

Bukovica

Muzej 1247

Čekanje

Lovćen-cesta

Bojanovica
spilja

Kosijeri

Košarica

Košarice

Bokovo

Jabuca

Gnevi Do

Donji Kraj

Relief 927
Crne Gore

Narodni muzej

Dobrsko
Selo

Vrba

4.5

Krstar

Dugi Do

Dubovik

Bajice

Tabla

Palace Biliarda
(672)

Bogorodičin
manastir

(571)

Lipska
Pecina

Cek

Sv.Matija

Sv.Ivan

AMS

Kotor

Sv.Nikola

Sv.Tripun

Skalijan

Niegoš
mauzolej

Vuči Do

Žanjev Do

Jezerski vrh

Miloševa pečina

Martinovići

Cetinje 8

Bjeloši
(884)

Očinići

819

Muo

Pomorski
muzej

Bogdašići

926

Strovnik 1660

1749

Mali
Bostur

park

Ugnji

Vrelo

2-3

Kavač

Trojka
228

Odoljen

Mirac

Dub

6.5

Dolovi

Ivanova Korita
(1264)

5.5

1305

Lovćen

1414

Obzovica

30

IĐSKO
polje

E80

2

Sutvara

Pelinovo

Naljezići
(372)

Šišići

Poda

Prijeradi

Goliš
1046

Gornji-

Kološun

1474

Majstori

Đurđevac

1282

Kosmač

Martinovići

Uglješić

Sv. Đorđe

Lješević

256

Radoanović

Bratešići

Bogetić

Pobori

Stanjević

Vrbice

Podmaini

286

Bečići

P

Du

Grabovac

Bigovo

Vranovići

Prčja glava
409

Pobrđe

Ukropci

Gorovići

Donji-
Lastva

Jadranska
magistrala

Podostrog

Maini
Boreti

Miločer

Kučice

Glavatičići

E65

19

Kubasi

Rodlastva

416

Dubovica

Prijevor

Budva

AMS

Hotel Miločer

Sveti Stefan
(28) GOLUBIN

Rt Žukovac

Kovači
425

Glavati

Sv.
Jovran

Gorica
364

Prijevor

389

ŠKOLJIĆ

SV. NIKOLA

6

Popović

Višnjevo

Kunjići

307

Gorica

Jaz

Jaz

Rt Mogren

SV. NIKOLA

Zagora

Krimovice
(196)

Sv. Andrija

141

Trsteno

Sv. Nikola

Rt Platamuni

4 km

2.49 mi

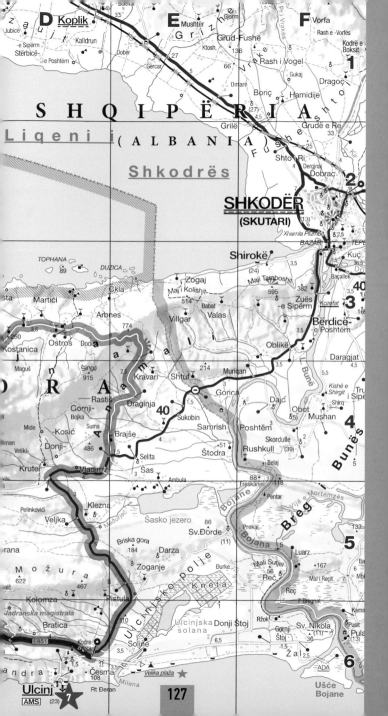

KEY TO ROAD ATLAS

Motorway · Toll junction · Toll station · Junction with number · Motel · Restaurant · Snackbar · Filling-station · Parking place with and without WC	Trento · 11	Autobahn · Gebührenpflichtige Anschlussstelle · Gebührenstelle · Anschlussstelle mit Nummer · Rasthaus mit Übernachtung · Raststätte · Kleinraststätte · Tankstelle · Parkplatz mit und ohne WC
Motorway under construction and projected with expected date of opening	Datum — Date	Autobahn in Bau und geplant mit Datum der voraussichtlichen Verkehrsübergabe
Dual carriageway (4 lanes)		Zweibahnige Straße (4-spurig)
Trunk road · Road numbers	14 E45	Fernverkehrsstraße · Straßennummern
Important main road		Wichtige Hauptstraße
Main road · Tunnel · Bridge	)=(	Hauptstraße · Tunnel · Brücke
Minor roads		Nebenstraßen
Track · Footpath		Fahrweg · Fußweg
Tourist footpath (selection)		Wanderweg (Auswahl)
Main line railway		Eisenbahn mit Fernverkehr
Rack-railway, funicular		Zahnradbahn, Standseilbahn
Aerial cableway · Chair-lift		Kabinenschwebebahn · Sessellift
Car ferry · Passenger ferry		Autofähre · Personenfähre
Shipping route		Schifffahrtslinie
Nature reserve · Prohibited area		Naturschutzgebiet · Sperrgebiet
National park · natural park · Forest		Nationalpark · Naturpark · Wald
Road closed to motor vehicles	X X X X	Straße für Kfz. gesperrt
Toll road		Straße mit Gebühr
Road closed in winter	XII-II	Straße mit Wintersperre
Road closed or not recommended for caravans		Straße für Wohnanhänger gesperrt bzw. nicht empfehlenswert
Tourist route · Pass	Weinstraße · 1510	Touristenstraße · Pass
Scenic view · Panoramic view · Route with beautiful scenery		Schöner Ausblick · Rundblick · Landschaftlich bes. schöne Strecke
Spa · Swimming pool		Heilbad · Schwimmbad
Youth hostel · Camping site		Jugendherberge · Campingplatz
Golf-course · Ski jump		Golfplatz · Sprungschanze
Church · Chapel		Kirche im Ort, freistehend · Kapelle
Monastery · Monastery ruin		Kloster · Klosterruine
Synagogue · Mosque		Synagoge · Moschee
Palace, castle · Ruin		Schloss, Burg · Schloss-, Burgruine
Tower · Radio-, TV-tower		Turm · Funk-, Fernsehturm
Lighthouse · Power station		Leuchtturm · Kraftwerk
Waterfall · Lock		Wasserfall · Schleuse
Important building · Market place, area		Bauwerk · Marktplatz, Areal
Arch. excavation, ruins · Mine		Ausgrabungs- u. Ruinenstätte · Bergwerk
Dolmen · Menhir · Nuraghe		Dolmen · Menhir · Nuraghen
Cairn · Military cemetery		Hünen-, Hügelgrab · Soldatenfriedhof
Hotel, inn, refuge · Cave		Hotel, Gasthaus, Berghütte · Höhle
Culture Picturesque town · Elevation	**WIEN** (171)	**Kultur** Malerisches Ortsbild · Ortshöhe
Worth a journey	★★ **MILANO**	Eine Reise wert
Worth a detour	★ **TEMPLIN**	Lohnt einen Umweg
Worth seeing	**Andermatt**	Sehenswert
Landscape Worth a journey	★★ **Las Cañadas**	**Landschaft** Eine Reise wert
Worth a detour	★ **Texel**	Lohnt einen Umweg
Worth seeing	**Dikti**	Sehenswert
Trips & Tours		**Ausflüge & Touren**
The perfect route		**Perfekte Route**
MARCO POLO Highlight	★1	**MARCO POLO Highlight**

INDEX

This index lists all places, destinations, mountains, rivers and persons featured in this guide. Numbers in bold indicate a main entry.

WRITE TO US

e-mail: info@marcopologuides.co.uk

Did you have a great holiday?
Is there something on your mind?
Whatever it is, let us know!
Whether you want to praise, alert us to errors or give us a personal tip – MARCO POLO would be pleased to hear from you.
We do everything we can to provide the very latest information for your trip.

Nevertheless, despite all of our authors' thorough research, errors can creep in. MARCO POLO does not accept any liability for this. Please contact us by e-mail or post.

MARCO POLO Travel Publishing Ltd
Pinewood, Chineham Business Park
Crockford Lane, Chineham
Basingstoke, Hampshire RG24 8AL
United Kingdom

PICTURE CREDITS
Cover photograph: Laif: Zahn (Bay of Kotor, Perast)
D. Antonović (1 bottom), M. Braunger (front flap left, 3 bottom, 39, 52, 69, 84/85, 92, 98); R. Freyer (3 top, 10/11, 12/13, 28/29, 29, 44, 56, 64/65, 110, 129); Huber: Gräfenhain (41, 50), Grandadam (26 left), Johanna Huber (30 top, 30 bottom), Pavan (2 bottom, 48/49); © istockphoto.com: CBCK-Christine (16 top); © istockphoto.com: GoodLifeStudio (17 bottom); G. Knoll (3 centre 8, 9, 27, 28, 36, 61, 63, 66, 70, 73, 76/77, 81, 89, 101); Laif: Henseler (front flap right, 2 centre bottom, 32/33, 43, 47), Zahn (1 top, 100/101); Laif/Hemis: Frilet (96/97); Look: Diomedia (34, 82); mauritius images: Alamy (2 top, 2 centre top, 4, 6, 7, 15, 21, 22/23, 24/25, 74, 78, 86, 105), Flüeler (94), Harding (59), Photoshot (55, 104 top); R. Maier/BM (5, 102, 103); C. Nowak (26 right, 102/103, 104 bottom, 118/119); Queen of Montenegro (17 top); Igor Rakcevic (16 centre); T. Stankiewicz (18/19); TOP LINE MARKETING (16 bottom); Transit Archiv: Nowak (90/91), Rotting (100/101)

1st Edition 2014
Worldwide Distribution: Marco Polo Travel Publishing Ltd, Pinewood, Chineham Business Park, Crockford Lane, Basingstoke, Hampshire RG24 8AL, United Kingdom. E-mail: sales@marcopolouk.com
© MAIRDUMONT GmbH & Co. KG, Ostfildern
Chief editor: Marion Zorn
Authors: Danja Antonović, Markus Bickel; editor: Felix Wolf
Programme supervision: Ann-Katrin Kutzner, Nikolai Michaelis
Picture editor: Gabriele Forst
What's hot: wunder media, Munich
Cartography road atlas & pull-out map: © MAIRDUMONT, Ostfildern
Design: milchhof : atelier, Berlin; Front cover, pull-out map cover, page 1: factor product munich
Translated from German by Robert Scott McInnes; editor of the English edition: Margaret Howie, fullproof.co.za
Prepress: M. Feuerstein, Wigel
Phrase book in cooperation with Ernst Klett Sprachen GmbH, Stuttgart, Editorial by Pons Wörterbücher

DOS & DON'TS ✋

Here are a few things you should look out for in Montenegro

DON'T WEAR SHOES IN MOSQUES

Spontaneous invitations to visit the mosque are quite common in small Muslim communities. Do what the Muslims do and remove your shoes off before you enter! If you visit a church or monastery, make sure you are not too casually dressed. By the way, members of the Orthodox faith leave religious places backwards – with their eyes fixed on the icons.

DON'T ASK QUESTIONS ABOUT LANGUAGE AND RELIGION

Montenegro is a multicultural country: Serbs, Albanians, Croatians and Bosnians live here – less than half of the population consider themselves Montenegrins. The situation is complicated and disagreements over language and nation continue. The question of religion is no less complicated. If you get into a conversation with one of the locals, talk about the weather – that is much less problematic.

DO OBEY THE SPEED LIMIT

It can be annoying when buses and trucks hold up traffic and you are forced to putter along behind them. If this happens, don't be tempted to step on the accelerator rather try to relax and drive slowly, a safer option on the winding roads in Montenegro. And, there are radar traps and police everywhere to make sure you adhere to the speed limit.

DO FIRST AGREE ON A RATE FOR YOUR TAXI

There are plenty of taxis – especially in the resort towns on the coast – but not all of the drivers are honest. A taxi meter plays no role, the price you agree on before you set out is the real charge so before you get into a taxi you must negotiate the fare. Most of the drivers speak a smattering of English. If you plan to go on a longer trip, ask various drivers at the taxi rank what they charge for the ride.

DON'T UNDERESTIMATE THE BLACK MOUNTAIN

The mountainous north is still something of an insiders' tip. But the weather can be unpredictable at an altitude of 1500m/5000ft, and the paths are not always that well marked. This makes it a good idea go on hikes in groups of at least three and take a mountain guide with you. Always check the weather report before you set out and make sure you let the people you are staying with know where you are going. And, just to be sure, take the telephone number of your hotel with you.

DON'T DRINK TAP WATER

Many towns and villages – especially on the coast – have the so-called 'technical water' and it is not potable. It is best to play it safe and stick to bottled mineral water.